Dear Medha,

Keep inspiring us
with your Fun-loving
Style !

Allia
July 2015

THE
POWER
OF
Understanding
PEOPLE

THE KEY TO **STRENGTHENING RELATIONSHIPS,**
INCREASING SALES, AND **ENHANCING**
ORGANIZATIONAL PERFORMANCE

DAVE MITCHELL

WILEY

For general information about our other products and services, please contact our Customer Care Department within the United States at (800) 762-2974, outside the United States at (317) 572-3993 or fax (317) 572-4002.

Wiley publishes in a variety of print and electronic formats and by print-on-demand. Some material included with standard print versions of this book may not be included in e-books or in print-on-demand. If this book refers to media such as a CD or DVD that is not included in the version you purchased, you may download this material at http://booksupport.wiley.com. For more information about Wiley products, visit www.wiley.com.

Library of Congress Cataloging-in-Publication Data:

Mitchell, Dave, 1961-
  The power of understanding people : the key to strengthening relationships, increasing sales, and enhancing organizational performance/Dave Mitchell.
     pages cm
  Includes index.
   ISBN 978-1-118-72683-9 (cloth); ISBN 978-1-118-72689-1 (ebk);
ISBN 978-1-118-72688-4 (ebk)
  1. Customer relations. 2. Customer services. 3. Interpersonal relations. I. Title.
HF5415.5.M578 2013
  650.1′3—dc23
                                                                            2013034150

10 9 8 7 6 5 4 3 2 1

Contents

Preface

This book is the result of a lifetime of fascination with human behavior.

"The world would be a wonderful place if it weren't for people," exhaled my father. He had just dealt with an unhappy customer who, in my father's words, "didn't just chew my ass out; he chewed around it and let it drop out."

I must have heard my father—who had a flair for both profanity and cliché—utter that first sentence a hundred times growing up. He sold appliances and heating and air-conditioning systems in a sleepy little town in rural Illinois. I learned—first from him, and eventually throughout life—that any job that requires you to make your living satisfying the general public's needs will involve both good days and bad ones.

My dad was a good salesperson and more than competent at building rapport with a wide variety of people. Still, the stress of earning money based on making people happy—people with different expectations and diverse lifestyles—was a constant part of his life. Even as a kid, I was aware of the efforts Dale Mitchell took to build successful relationships. In many ways, long before my education and career choices, the seeds of my interest in human behavior were sewn working in that little store in Greenup, Illinois.

This book is the culmination of years of informal observation, academic research, and career responsibilities both inside the corporate world and as an international speaker, author, and consultant. It also contains my personal opinions, based on practical experiences that, although not supported by formal evidence, have worked for me. It is designed to be both entertaining and informative and is organized around my philosophy of learning: the three elements of *absorb, connect,* and *apply,* depicted in Figure P.1.

Absorb activities expose you to information that you may or may not already know. Think of sitting through a teacher's lecture or watching a television documentary. You watch with interest (hopefully) and allow the content to enter your working

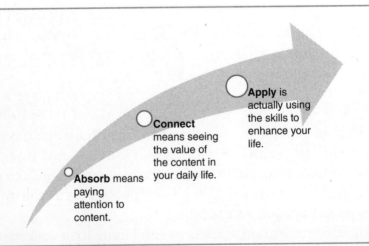

FIGURE P.1 A Simple Model for the Transfer of Learning

memory. This is the first step of learning: paying attention. If you are reading this book after attending my seminar, you are experiencing a valuable reinforcement of the initial absorb activity that you experienced at the live presentation. For those of you who are experiencing this content for the first time, reading this book is your initial absorb activity. That works, too (although I would really appreciate you putting in a good word for me with the person in your organization that hires speakers!).

Of course, absorbing information is only the beginning of the learning process. As anyone who sat through a high school physics class and later graduated with a degree in liberal arts can attest, paying attention to information does not equate to *learning* it. Another step is required: *connecting* this new information to something in your life that gives it value. In essence, you need to ask yourself, "How can I *use* this information?" I approach this in two ways in the following pages. First, you will take an assessment to determine your interactive style and learn about how you think relative to other ways of thinking. Nothing connects with us more than learning about ourselves, am I right? (I know I love doing all those simple surveys in *Cosmo*. And I will now turn in my man card.)

But seriously, self-discovery is a huge *connect* activity. I've also sprinkled stories and examples of situations involving the interaction between diverse styles throughout the entire book. These reflect common life experiences both at work and at home, during which our differences manifest themselves in our behaviors. We all have found ourselves in situations in which we felt very comfortable communicating with others. Conversely, we have been in situations that were . . . umm . . . clunky, to say the least. These stories are meant to capture these moments. Hopefully, when you read these examples, you will say to yourself, "OMG! That happened to me just last week." That is a connect moment when you recognize the value of the principles and how you can use them in your life.

However, paying attention and identifying the content's value is still not enough to complete the transfer of learning. For example, I often watch cooking shows on television and think to myself, "That would be so cool to make for my wife." Umm, yeah. Let's just say that I am more proficient at wine selection and dish washing than creating culinary masterpieces. That's because I don't actually practice preparing that food. This is the final piece of the transfer of learning: *applying* the information. This book's latter chapters contain ways to apply the content relative to leadership, selling, customer service, and personal relationships. Of course, just reading about how to apply this information isn't the same as actually applying it. But after much thought, I decided that physically coming to your home or work and holding you accountable for applying the concepts was creepy. However, I am available for that aforementioned corporate speaking event. (Too much? Sorry.)

Anyway, that's how the book is organized: Absorb the content, connect it to your life, then apply it to enhance your leadership, selling, service, and/or professional and personal relationship skills. Rinse and repeat as necessary.

Introduction

We Are All Delusional!

"Why in the world would you do that?" Haven't we all asked ourselves that question when we witness behavior that makes us scratch our head? And not just about strangers either. Our own spouses, siblings, parents, children, friends, and colleagues have stunned us with their actions as well. Why is this? Why do human beings with the same biophysiological equipment, the same sensory receptors, behave in such diverse ways when in the same settings? I mean, how is it possible that my wife is not completely emotionally immersed in the drama of a University of Illinois basketball game in the same way I am? Why should she be surprised at the expletives I express when my beloved players miss an easy basket in a close game against Michigan State? Oh, the humanity!

The key to understanding the mysteries of human behavior involves a concept called *metacognition*, which literally means "thinking about thinking." For the purposes of this book, I will use the term to mean metacognitive self-awareness. There are other slightly different definitions for metacognition and metacognitive self-awareness, so let me clearly articulate mine: Metacognitive self-awareness is *an understanding of how our life experiences have shaped our cognitive schemas* —which, in turn, determine how we derive meaning from our reality. (I promise that the entire book won't be so painfully clinical.)

Okay, so you're wondering, "What in the world are schemas?" Well, schemas (again, for the purpose of my definition) are mental structures that provide us with a way to organize and derive meaning from our experiences. They are ways we apply our knowledge and assumptions. And they are the core of perception.

Let me give you a couple of examples. Let's say your earliest childhood memories of dogs involved the loyal, fun, and cuddly family pet Kibbles. You played with Kibbles, lay next to him, and often stroked Kibbles's fur for comfort. You create a schema for dogs that organizes your ideas around these positive experiences with Kibbles.

Now, let's say you have a friend who did not grow up around a dog. In fact, he was once bitten by a dog when he was a child. Your friend forms a schema that dogs are unpredictable and potentially mean.

Later, you and your friend are walking down the street when a stray dog suddenly appears. You, with your schema that dogs are positive, probably approach the dog to see if it has a name tag. Your friend freezes, looks around for an owner, and avoids any contact with the dog. Same dog, two distinctly different reactions.

There are actually *three* realities occurring in this experience. First is what I call absolute or objective reality, the version of reality that represents the actual dog in this scenario. Absolute reality exists only as a concept for people. It is the version of reality that is not influenced by our own experiences, which have created our personal knowledge, preferences, prejudices—our schemas. Because we all have had experiences and have therefore developed schemas, absolute reality is not the reality within which we live.

The other two realities are you and your friend's "delusions." In your delusion, the stray dog is a cuddly creature in need of assistance. In your friend's delusion, the dog is a dangerous creature that should be avoided. One of you may be closer to the absolute reality than the other, but neither of you are operating completely within it. You are each creating a reality driven by your own schemas.

SOCIOCULTURAL SCHEMAS

If you consider that no other person on the planet has shared your collection of experiences, then you soon realize that your cognitive schemas are unique to you. And, if you further consider that your schemas determine how you derive meaning, you then realize that your delusion is also unique to you. Finally, because delusion drives behavior and we are all uniquely deluded . . . well, you can see the trouble that ensues when we anticipate that *anyone* will behave according to our expectations. This is troubling when you consider the 7 billion people on the planet, each living in his or her own Private Idaho, if you will, and acting on a desire to connect with one another. Is it any wonder we are so stressed out?!

Thankfully, civilized society provides us with a number of shared experiences. These are often driven by ideology, things such as religion, government, and education. A simple example from the U.S. educational system is the alphabet. If you were educated in the United States and English is your first language, you likely learned the alphabet using two distinct academic schemas. First, your teacher chunked the 26 symbols into groups of two, three, or four characters. You spent some time on ABCD, then went on to EFG, HIJK, and so on. Second, you learned the melody that kept those individual chunks in order. Now, if a group of individuals learned to recite the alphabet using that approach, they all share a reality. If I ask each member of this group to recite the alphabet, even many years after the experience of learning it, each member will think about it in the same way that the rest of the group would at that moment: Everyone in the group would group the letters and sing the same melody. They have a shared sociocultural schema for the alphabet. However, someone who did not learn the alphabet in this manner does not share this schema.

Sociocultural schemas are vital, because they provide groups of people with a shared way of deriving meaning. Although individuals will still have a unique delusion, the sociocultural schemas provide some common ground that allows them to have a better collective understanding. Unfortunately, although sociocultural schemas may unite some cultures, they will likely divide others. Entire wars are fought over differences in religious, political, and cultural schemas. However, that discussion is for another book. In this book, we look at the one globally unifying set of schemas—species-level schemas, if you will. I call these schemas *interactive styles*.

INTERACTIVE STYLES

Have you ever met a total stranger, talked to that person for a few minutes, and said to yourself, "I dig you like a ditch?" You know that feeling; it's an immediate connection that you somehow achieve with certain people. And that feeling increases your self-efficacy, a term that essentially means "situational confidence." I like to compare it to a baseball player who is feeling comfortable in the batter's box and who possesses a certain surety that he can hit any pitch thrown to him. Someone who has high self-efficacy tends to execute his or her skill set at its highest level. If that individual has a competent skill set, then you can expect to have a successful outcome.

Let's say you are a sales professional. You meet your prospective client for the first time and immediately hit it off. You both get each other, and communication flows comfortably. You experience both relaxation and confidence—that feeling of high self-efficacy. You successfully identify the potential client's needs and frame your products and services in a way that really resonates. And because you have done such a good job of identifying the client's needs—and displaying your products' and service's value—the client buys. You reach a mutually successful outcome.

But what if you meet that new client and your first reaction is, "You . . . might be the anti-Christ!" Come on; we all know it happens on occasion. Some people just rub us the wrong way. And you know what? They probably feel the exact same way about us.

This situation initiates the exact opposite chain reaction to the one described earlier. When you're attempting to make a sale and the initial rapport is poor, self-efficacy drops. You get nervous and uncomfortable, which in turn affects your skills. Now, instead of accurately and efficiently identifying your client's needs and bridging them to your capabilities, you begin to spray and pray or, as sales professionals colorfully say, show up and throw up. That is, you sling all the features and benefits of your products at the client in the hopes that something—*anything*—excites him or her. And this ineffective approach causes the client to pass on your products.

When you don't consider metacognition—and when you don't have any training on how to recognize behavioral cues and adjust quickly within a given situation—you're leaving your communication success to chance. Obviously, to maximize your effectiveness as a leader, sales professional, or customer service provider, you want to experience far more situations like the first example. To do so, you must understand and apply metacognitive skills and answer questions such as, "What exactly is this phenomenon?" and "How do I improve my skills in communication?" The answers to both of these questions and countless others start by understanding interactive styles.

Some of the greatest minds in history have offered models for explaining human beings' iconic traits. Hippocrates, Galen, Plato, Aristotle, and countless other philosophers noticed that despite our many unique behaviors, patterns could still be observed. These "types" were most comprehensively articulated by Carl Jung in his 1921 book *Psychological Types*. This book served as the inspiration for the Myers-Briggs Type Indicator, one of the most widely used personality assessments in the world.

For the record, I put more stock in people's traits than in certain types. It is a subtle distinction, but one that I believe is important. When you take an assessment, you get very black and white results. Although this kind of distinction is useful, we can learn a great deal as well by looking at the continuum upon which the scores fall and the relationships between scores. These data provide more nuance and complexity to the results. Of course, it also makes them more complicated, which probably explains why most evaluations stop at the type. It would be a daunting task to write a book or deliver a training session that addresses the numerous elements involved within the continuums and relationships. And working at the type level does allow for many important insights. So this book will explore interactive styles using type. If you want more nuances, call me to schedule a training session for your organization. (Okay, no more self-promotion. I promise.)

The aforementioned great minds from philosophy and psychology have noticed that regardless of the individual and sociocultural-based schemas that influence our delusions, all humans seem to organize ideas in similar ways. This allows human beings to ultimately behave as pack animals despite having unique delusions. I believe the four schemas serve to unify and protect us from a tendency to destroy one another because of our varied realities. Minimally, they provide what

Jung called the collective unconscious. Their presence gives all of humanity a commonality of interpretation of life experiences . . . like a shade or a hue that colors our individual delusion and softens its uniqueness—the delusion of humankind, so to speak. This book will explore these four schemas and how they affect our ability to lead, sell, service, and communicate in general. The applications stretch beyond our professional life and into our personal relationships.

Rapport, relationships, communication, and many other elements of the human existence are significantly affected by this concept of interactive style. Like other schemas, it is affected by our life experiences and consequently can evolve and even change drastically over time. Interactive style also affects an individual's intrinsic needs and can therefore help determine a person's motivation and resiliency. By understanding the concept of interactive style, we can improve all forms of relationships, leadership, selling skills, and customer service—just like in the sales example I used previously. Interactive style plays a critical role in any dynamic that involves communication and provides essential information related to stress management.

The complicating factor is that although we all possess the same interactive styles, we use them differently. Our individual preferences are formed by our distinctive life experiences. This is why interactive style can both unify and frustrate us. To understand this, let me provide an analogy.

Imagine that you and all other humans are born with a toolbox containing four tools: a hammer, a screwdriver, pliers, and a wrench. The purposes of the toolbox are to establish rapport with other people and to aid in communication and understanding; the four tools help us accomplish this. Because each of us has the same box and the same four tools, we should be joining hands and singing "We Are the World" right? Yeah, not so much. You see, after birth we all have our own unique experiences that affect the ways in which we develop our schemas, including the ones for interactive style. So over time, the four tools begin to fall into a different order of preference for each person. Maybe it is the influence of one or both parents, maybe it's a sibling or a friend, or perhaps teachers or a series of other life events that shape this preference. Heck, there may even be a DNA-related element. It's hard to determine whether you have an ingrained style preference from birth. You are not a particularly good communicator as a newborn, and research interviews tend to be frustrating for both parties. So by the time you can articulate your thoughts, you have already been influenced by your environment.

Anyway, for whatever reason—but largely because of your experiences—you begin to have a preferred tool, a secondary tool, a tertiary tool, and a . . . um . . . quaternary tool. Your toolbox now has depth (top tool to bottom tool), and that depth equates to stress. Tools on the top are accompanied by very little stress, whereas those on the bottom bring you more stress.

Let's further imagine that I am a hammer guy; my primary preference for interactive style is my hammer. I experience life through a hammer schema. My behavior is hammer-influenced. I relate best to hammer people. As I walk around the planet, I keep my hammer at the top of my toolbox. When I meet another hammer person, let's say his name is Bill, I choose the interactive tool that I believe is most appropriate for this situation. I hammer on Bill, and it goes well. Bill gets me; I get Bill. My self-efficacy is enhanced, and I am able to better execute my skills. Whatever the desired outcome (selling, leading, customer service, or just a fulfilling chat), I will most likely achieve it.

I continue down my life path and meet a screwdriver person. We'll call her Sally. I choose the tool that I believe is most appropriate for this situation. That tool is . . . the hammer. What? Why would I choose a hammer when I am dealing with a screwdriver person? The answer is simple: In *my* interpretation of reality, all situations are best served by the hammer, simply because I am a hammer person. It is my preferred tool. Unless I engage in some serious metacognition and think about how I think, my natural tendency is to use the interactive style schema that is most comfortable for me.

So I hammer on Sally, and it doesn't go well. There's a disconnect between us. But because humans are pack animals, I want to connect with this person. That intrinsic need to bond with other members of my species will motivate me to endure a little discomfort and seek a more effective tool. I go back to my toolbox and grab my secondary preference; let's say that tool is the screwdriver. (It wouldn't necessarily be, but for purposes of this illustration, let's assume that it is.) After having hammered ineffectively on Sally, I now have my screwdriver and . . . uh . . . um . . . errr . . . *twist*. I *twist* Sally. And now we are fine, because even though I am a hammer guy, I'm using the tool that works best in this situation: a good screwdriver.

Continuing with this analogy, I meet a wrench: Stanley. I choose the tool that I believe to be most appropriate for Stanley, and that tool is a hammer. When the hammer fails to work, I grab the screwdriver. Remember, it's my reality so I go in order of my comfort level. After having hammered and twisted Stanley, what happens next? "Well, Dave, clearly you will grab your tertiary tool, hopefully a wrench, right?"

Nope. I'll tell you what we usually do. Inside our head we say, "Whack job!" or "Freak show!" or some variation of terms that indicates that this person's behavior makes no sense to us and is therefore inappropriate—because it doesn't jibe with our reality. The person's behavior causes us stress, and we associate this stress with being wrong. We then blame the other person for creating this stressful experience.

Of course, the *objective* reality of this situation is that neither you nor the other person is a bad person; you are just different. But in your delusion, you experience it differently. In your mind, Stanley is a jerk. The stress you are experiencing originates from your own delusion, but because we externalize this stress, we assign its cause to the other person. The truth is, just like the dog in my earlier example, Stanley is just being Stanley. *You* are defining your interaction with him as stressful.

Again, this phenomenon affects relationships of all types. Marriages fail, clients are lost, customers are unsatisfied, and children are misunderstood—all because of this dynamic. The frustrating part of this concept is that we all have all the same tools, so we have the raw resources to successfully navigate each diverse style. And although that's true from an objective reality perspective, from a pragmatic and delusional perspective, we simply don't always do it.

The good news is we can learn to adjust our style more effectively with some knowledge and practice. It can still be irritating and exhausting, but you can develop better relationships of all types by mastering the skills outlined in this book. Yes—the people who annoy you now will continue to annoy you, but now you will know why and understand that it is not because they are bad people. You'll also know what to do to make the situation less stressful for you both, because, by the way, don't forget that you annoy them, too!

Now, because using tools is pretty ambiguous and not the least bit sexy, I actually describe the different interactive styles using a Hollywood theme. I have found that people remember these concepts better if they have names for the different types. I have been exposed to myriad assessments that use letters, colors, and descriptive names to define styles. Unfortunately, most of the results sounded like a viral infection to me. (When I was told I was an INFJ, I asked if we had caught it in time.) So I opted for movie characters for my approach. Why not? It's fun, memorable, and lighthearted; makes for the best educational experience; and fits perfectly with my company's motto: "Laugh and Learn!"

HOLLYWOOD STYLE!

At the end of this Introduction, you will find *The Power of Understanding People* Assessment. Completing it will give you an idea of the order of the tools in your toolbox. The following chapters examine each of the four iconic styles in detail, including how they communicate, what their intrinsic needs are, how you identify each one, and how you adjust to that particular style. The most practical application of the information will be to learn how to recognize the behavioral cues of each of these iconic styles and develop strategies to adjust to them when leading, selling, serving—really, doing any kind of interacting in both professional and personal situations.

After discussing each of the four iconic styles, we will delve more deeply into your results by identifying the iconic movie characters that are represented by the combination of primary and secondary styles. As an added benefit, you will also now have several credible recommendations for which actor should portray you when they film the motion picture about your life. Clearly, Brad Pitt for me, but the results aren't always based on physical likeness. (Are you laughing? Seriously, that hurts.)

A DISCLAIMER

Before we go too far, I want to make something very clear. Engaging in metacognition, actually thinking about how you think and challenging yourself to think differently than you are inclined to do, is very difficult. Our mind prefers to rely on schemas to extract meaning from things because, quite frankly, it is faster and easier. Many of my colleagues who are far smarter than I am would tell you that the whole concept of free will is a fallacy. They argue, quite convincingly, that your behavior will become predictable once you have created a thought process (schema) for dealing with life experiences. You will behave in each given circumstance in the exact same way that you have before. And although I understand this point, I respectfully disagree. I believe that we can use commitment and self-awareness to both change our schemas and situationally adjust them as needed. To change a schema is very difficult and may require years of effort, but to *adjust* a schema in given circumstances—particularly as it relates to interactive style—is much easier. Our intrinsic need for human connection aids our ability to adjust our interactive style based on a certain situation, and the extrinsic rewards surrounding this dynamic can motivate us even further. If building rapport with someone benefits me in some way—for example, getting a commission, receiving a higher service satisfaction rating, or enhancing a relationship—then I'll be highly motivated to situationally adjust my interactive style. This book will help you learn how to execute this adjustment.

THE ASSESSMENT

"Blah, blah, blah . . . when do I get to learn what movie character I am?" I get it. You bought the book because you wanted to learn about your own interactive style. We humans are self-centered, after all, and you can gain some real value from enhancing your metacognitive awareness. Just keep in mind that the true enrichment comes from understanding *others'* delusions. This is how you begin to improve your relationships.

Let me give you a few important caveats about the assessment. Although there are no right or wrong answers, there certainly can be correct or incorrect answers. Confused? Well, although every style is valuable and valid, your results will be accurate only if you answer the assessment honestly. I remember doing a seminar for about 200 people in a lovely corporate training facility when, 2 hours into the event, a young lady raised her hand. "My results don't sound accurate," she offered. I looked at her and said, "Well, it's a self-assessment." (It's a thought joke.)

Don't overanalyze your responses or complete the assessment in a way you think you *should* complete it. In other words, don't "should" on yourself. Shoulding on yourself will invalidate the results and result in an inaccurate style being reported for you, which won't help guide your interactions with others at all. If you find yourself overthinking a response, chances are you are about to should on yourself. You certainly don't want to do that.

You may also find some of the scenarios difficult to rank. Don't worry about that. Go with your first reaction.

Okay, go ahead and do the assessment. I'll be here when you get back with your Hollywood movie character. (That's my favorite part!)

The Power of Understanding People

Name_____ Date_____

Below, there are 12 sections, each with 4 statements labeled "a," "b," "c," and "d." After you read statements a, b, c, and d, choose the one that you like the best and put a "1" in the box next to the letter that matches that statement; put a "2" in the box of the statement you like the next best; a "3" in the next; and a "4" in the one you like the least.

a. Your favorite restaurant or vacation spot
b. Family and/or friends
c. A new place or situation
d. A competitive and/or learning situation
  a. ☐   b. ☐   c. ☐   d. ☐

a. A well-structured company
b. A people-oriented company
c. A creative company
d. A fast-growing company
  a. ☐   b. ☐   c. ☐   d. ☐

a. A job or project that is well organized
b. A job or project that benefits others
c. A job or project that is different and exciting
d. A job or project that is mentally stimulating
  a. ☐   b. ☐   c. ☐   d. ☐

a. A dependable relationship
b. A meaningful relationship
c. An exciting relationship
d. A respect-based relationship
  a. ☐   b. ☐   c. ☐   d. ☐

a. Rewards based on quality
b. Rewards based on teamwork
c. Rewards based upon originality of ideas
d. Rewards based upon merit and achievement
  a. ☐   b. ☐   c. ☐   d. ☐

a. Feeling secure
b. Being appreciated
c. Doing something interesting
d. Being independent
  a. ☐   b. ☐   c. ☐   d. ☐

a. A well-played ball game
b. A moving emotional experience
c. A new and different experience
d. A competitive experience   a. ☐   b. ☐   c. ☐   d. ☐

a. A task that one can see or touch
b. A task that makes one feel good
c. A task that calls upon one's imagination
d. A task that requires logical reasoning   a. ☐   b. ☐   c. ☐   d. ☐

a. Consistent work
b. Harmonious work
c. Changing work
d. Efficient work   a. ☐   b. ☐   c. ☐   d. ☐

a. Being accurate
b. Being compassionate
c. Being innovative
d. Being productive   a. ☐   b. ☐   c. ☐   d. ☐

a. A meeting to discuss details
b. A meeting to discuss feelings
c. A meeting to discuss ideas
d. A meeting to discuss results   a. ☐   b. ☐   c. ☐   d. ☐

a. Knowing the directions
b. Working with a great team
c. Discovering something new
d. Being done with a project   a. ☐   b. ☐   c. ☐   d. ☐

TOTAL   a ☐   b ☐   c ☐   d ☐

When you are through ranking the items, add up all the numbers in column a and total them at the bottom of the column. Then do the same for columns b, c, and d. © Copyright 1997, 2004 the Leadership Difference, Inc.

Book us for your next event: Dave@theLeadershipDifference.com

www.theleadershipdifference.com

303-816-2658

Chapter 1 Understanding Romantics and Warriors

It's Feelings versus Logic for These Styles

If your lowest score is in column b, you are a Romantic. Now, there are three distinct types of Romantics (just as there are for all four of the styles), and we will explore these when we examine the 12 Hollywood movie characters. For now, let's focus on the similarities that exist between all Romantics.

Romantics' style is based on sensitivity to emotion. They live in a delusion comprised of feelings and experience emotions more palpably than the other three styles. Imagine that we each have six senses—the traditional five plus one more that our life experiences (not our DNA) have created. The Romantics' sixth sense is in perceiving the emotional content of their environment.

A Romantic can walk into a room, see someone, and correctly proclaim, "They are *not* happy," without even talking to the other person. Non-Romantics might ask, "How do you know? You haven't talked to anyone." "I can just tell; the anger is thick in here," the Romantic responds. Somehow, the Romantic's life experiences have made him or her more adept at recognizing feelings. Perhaps the Romantic is more attuned to nonverbal communication elements or has actually developed a sixth sense of emotion. Whatever the reason, Romantics live in a feeling world.

Romantics' primary desire is for world peace. "Why can't we all just get along?" they wonder. If we could just join hands and sing "We Are the World," they would be happy. They tend to be tactful and diplomatic. They often sacrifice their own needs to make others happy and keep the emotional environment positive. They tend to avoid conflict and spend a great deal of time packaging the message when delivering bad news. You can expect Romantics to wrap the negative in pretty paper with a bow to take as much pain from the news as possible. And if Romantics hurt someone's feelings, you can rest assured that they meant to do it. They may say, "I am so sorry; I didn't mean to hurt your feelings," but yeah, that's not true. Romantics know exactly how their behaviors will affect emotions.

If your lowest score is in column d, you are a Warrior. Warriors are not going for world peace; they are going for world domination. They know there will be casualties and believe we should start by killing the stupid people. Warriors do not suffer fools gladly and have a logical sensitivity. You probably have never heard of this type of sensitivity, but it's like seeing the shortest path to a desired outcome. I imagine Warriors as possessing a time invested/value received scale inside their heads. For Warriors, the more time invested, the greater the value received will need to be. By this measure, if Warriors can minimize time invested, they take pressure of the required value received—and tend to put pressure on things to speed up as a result. Warriors like efficiency, results, and to be *done*. The quickest route to the outcome is the one they prefer. Anything that takes them off this path increases time invested and becomes irritating. Things such as conference calls, unnecessary meetings, and small talk all can annoy them a great deal.

"Pretty sure you don't care about my weekend, and I certainly don't care about yours. Let's go to work," probably runs through the mind of every Warrior leader on each Monday morning.

These two very different sensitivities affect the way these styles communicate. Warriors are direct communicators because that's the quickest way to send a message. The words convey the entirety of the meaning. Don't try to read anything into what they said or find some hidden, unexpressed message; what they say is what they mean.

Romantics are indirect communicators; the words they say mean nothing. Well, not *nothing*, but the words actually convey very little of the true meaning. The real message is in their left eyebrow . . . or their tone, word choice, accompanying facial expressions, posture, pace, how hard they place a plate down on the table, and so on. Fellow Romantics understand this communication technique, but other styles . . . not so much. This can be a source of great frustration for Romantics. But when two Romantics communicate, the meaning is obvious. Two Warriors can beat each other about the head and upper body, assault one another verbally, and then go have a beer together—and the only person who is upset by the exchange is the Romantic who witnessed it. Basically, Warriors have no idea what Romantics are trying to communicate, and Romantics think Warriors are angrier than they really are.

The two styles negotiate in very different ways. Romantics build relationships with the other party, endearing themselves as a friend. Their strategy is, "If the other party gets to know me well enough, they will give me a better deal. They will 'take care of me.'" I call this the *honor bar approach* to negotiation. It is based on trusting that the other person will do the right thing, because the two people involved have a relationship. In doing so, the Romantic avoids the potentially unpleasant emotional impact of conflict during negotiations.

Warriors, on the other hand, are aggressive negotiators. They don't trust a deal that they didn't work hard to get, and it is crucial that they win in the end. They are competitive, so it would be difficult for them to imagine that you would just *give* them the best deal up front. We'll talk more about the practical application of this issue in later chapters, but there is a more figurative application for these tendencies, too. It relates to something called *intrinsic needs*.

Human behavior is motivated by two of types of needs: intrinsic and extrinsic. *Extrinsic* needs include things such as income, benefits, leisure time, and promotions. These issues can influence performance levels but are a less efficient and effective way to inspire behavior. Intrinsic needs are more powerful. I like to think of the difference like this. There are a couple of ways you can get your car to move. You can put fuel inside the tank and let the motor power the car, or you can push it. Clearly, you go a lot farther with a lot less effort using the former approach. Extrinsic rewards are like pushing the car; intrinsic rewards are like fueling the car from the inside.

Here's an example. Let's say that Chase is a Warrior. Chase is trying to finish a client project he is working on, but he needs a signed document before he can close the file. When he calls the client, the client tells Chase that he will fax the document right over to him. A fax—really? What is this, 1995? Chase is already aggravated, because now he has to find the fax machine and wait for the client to send over the document. Now Chase is in the mailroom stalking the fax machine like it's a wild animal. He is stomping around, sighing, and exclaiming to anyone within earshot that he can't believe he is waiting on a fax. A *FAX!*

Eventually, Chase notices that Marty has been in the mailroom the entire time. Marty is a Romantic. Chase thinks, "If Marty is going to be hanging out in here anyway, he might as well keep an eye out for my fax." This would allow Chase to go back to his office and be productive rather than waste time here. It's a no-brainer for Chase. Chase turns to Marty, "Hey Marty, I should be getting a fax any minute from a client. Would you mind grabbing it and putting it into my box when it comes in?"

Now, is this Marty's job? No. Does Marty do it? Yes. Why? When I ask this question during my seminars, the answers are usually, "because Marty is nice," or "Marty is a people pleaser," or some variation of that theme. All of those responses are accurate, but there is a darker, more sinister motivation for Marty that Romantics won't share with you. Marty wants Chase *gone*. Yep. Chase is a buzzkill for Marty. He is messing with Marty's mellow. So, if Marty can eliminate Chase and his toxic emotions from his environment simply by taking care of this fax, then it's a done deal!

Is there a fee for this service that Marty is providing? Yes. There is always a fee for a service, but notice that Marty did not negotiate any payment. That's because the Romantic Marty is using an honor bar approach. Any Romantic would know that there is a fee for this service, so he doesn't need to ask for payment. Payment will be provided. And that payment is appreciation. Appreciation is the Romantic style's currency—the intrinsic need of the Romantic community. Romantics are happy to self-sacrifice for the good of others, provided they are paid with some praise, some love. A little sugar, if you will. Romantics perform at their best in appreciation-abundant environments.

But does Chase pay Marty? Again, when I ask this question during my seminar, I generally receive a resounding, "*No!*" (Apparently, there are lots of angry Romantics out there.) The fact is, Chase *does* pay. Unfortunately, he pays using the wrong currency—the one that's consistent with *his* intrinsic need. And that is not appreciation for the Warrior: It is *independence*. Warriors operate under the principle, "Do you like my work? Yes? Then leave me alone!" No news is good news to the Warrior. If you do your job well, you are rewarded with *freedom*. So if Chase trusts Marty to take care of the fax, he will leave him alone.

Marty, however, views this independence in a very different way: He feels unappreciated and is now annoyed. As Marty sees it, Chase is in bad debt, and Marty is going to make a Romantic collection call. Here's how that works: Chase is walking one way down the hall, and Marty is coming toward him. Chase sees Marty and asks, "Hey Marty, how's it going?" "Fine," Marty replies in a clipped tone. There is no accompanying smile or reciprocated interest in Chase. All the Romantics who witness this know what "fine" means in this context. Marty just told Chase that the two of them have an issue and that the circle of trust has been broken. All the other Romantics notice immediately and start chatting, "What's up between Marty and Chase?"

But what does "fine" mean to Chase? It means Marty is fine. Remember: The words convey the entirety of meaning for a Warrior. In Chase's mind, he asked Marty how he was and Marty said fine. In fact, Chase thinks they had a particularly good conversation today. Sometimes Marty can be chatty, but today he was straight to the point. Chase didn't even break stride. Perfect! But for poor Marty, still no payment. Bad debt confirmed.

This brings us to the concept of the CTL container—something that I strongly believe will be viewed as my biggest contribution to applied cognitive psychology. Sure, it hasn't been acknowledged by the scientific community nor is it based on any valid research, but my experiences observing human behavior make me confident in its existence. CTL stands for crap tolerance level. Romantics have a huge CTL container but a very small spoon for emptying it. When Romantics feel that someone has taken them for granted, like Marty in the preceding example, they can place those emotions in the CTL container. Now, although it is a large container, it is not infinite. It has a lid. To put crap into the container, Romantics must open the lid. The lid is voice-activated using a key word. That word is often *whatever*. When you hear Romantics say, "You know what, whatever," their container is open and crap is being put in.

As Romantics' CTL containers reach their full capacity, subtle behavioral changes begin to occur. Romantics may not smile as much, may not take as great an interest in other people's lives, and may become a bit more edgy or sarcastic. They may place items on a dining table or desk with more force than usual. These changes are not immediately recognized by the other styles, only by fellow Romantics. But when fellow Romantics notice these changes, they realize instantly that their style brethren needs some help spooning out the crap. "Come on, everyone. Marty's container is full," they say as they all come running, each with their little spoon, to help Marty empty out his crap. This is called happy hour.

Actually, it is called *venting*. Venting is a very important element of Romantics' mental well-being. And because the source of the crap is often a Warrior, it is to them that they wish to vent. However, Warriors don't understand venting. You see, they have a tiny little CTL container. They don't store much crap. But they have a *big* ladle for emptying the container, which means they are always flinging crap. "Take your crap with you; I don't have any room for your crap." The concept of storing up crap for a ceremonial emptying event like venting is completely alien to Warriors. In fact, they don't call it venting. They call it whining. "Why would you complain about things and not want to fix them?" thinks the Warrior. Of course, this only leads to more crap for the Romantics.

Many Warriors have learned—either through seminars and resources like this book or from human resources professionals, attorneys, and marriage counselors—the importance of supporting Romantics in the venting process. Even when a Warrior has come to understand the importance of venting, he or she still often struggles with execution. Organizations and marriages are full of examples like this:

Marty (the Romantic) *knocks on Chase's office door*.
"Hey Chase, do you have a second?" This is Romantic

speak for, "My CTL container is full and most of its contents came from you, so I've arrived to empty it."

Chase (the Warrior) is sitting at his desk with a long to-do list, with "talk to Marty" nowhere on it. If he doesn't feel he has time or that talking to Marty is that important, he is very comfortable saying, "No, I am really busy. Catch me later." However, if Chase has been made aware of the importance of venting, then he will likely mentally survey his to-do list to determine the items that can be replaced with "talk to Marty." This reprioritizing of Chase's day will likely take about 3 seconds of time. During these 3 seconds, it would not be unusual for Chase to emit an audible sigh. It is the sigh of resignation that accompanies the realization that today will not be as productive as Chase had hoped. Ultimately, Chase responds with, <sigh> "Sure, come in." This is Warrior speak for "Sure, come in." (Remember, the words convey the entirety of the meaning.)

But what did Marty hear when Chase spoke those words? "No." Remember, the words mean little or nothing for Romantics. It was the *sigh* that imparted the majority of the message. And what does the sigh mean to Romantics? Well, roughly translated, "I would rather have a stick shoved in my eye than talk to you for the next 30 minutes." The miscommunication continues:

Marty responds to Chase by saying, "You know what? You obviously have more important things to do than talk with me right now." He pivots on his heel and walks away. In Romantic talk, Marty clearly said, "You just made a bad decision. Chase me down and drag me back into your office, because things will only get worse if my CTL container overflows!"

Chase thinks, "Sweet, dodged a bullet there. Marty's odd. He's like an antivampire. You invite him in, and he leaves. Oh well, back to my list."

As we will discover in the later chapters devoted to applying this information, learning how to successfully navigate the venting process is critical to leading and maintaining healthy personal relationships with Romantics.

Here's a question: Is it possible that a Romantic could meet, date, fall in love with, and marry a Warrior? It's not just possible; it's *likely!* If you are a Romantic or Warrior, you may have already made plans to give the assessment to your spouse. How could two such radically different styles of people be so attracted to each other? Why do opposites attract? Well, let me tell you what we know about love in cognitive psychology:

Nothing.

There doesn't seem to be any patterns that would lead us to conclude that compatibility is more attractive than complementary when it comes to the role of style in love. All I know is that many people report that it was love at first sight (or very quickly) when they met their future spouse. One glance and "BOOYAH, I am all about that." Other people report a more slow burn. They may have worked together for years without experiencing any romantic interest. Then, one day, they look at each other and say, "You know, in the right light, you are an attractive person. And I ain't getting any younger." BOOYAH.

In either situation, hormones and naturally produced substances such as dopamine, oxytocin, and pheromones all seem to be elevated—like a love cocktail. We experience a sort of love-driven euphoria during which we embrace our differences as people and think things like, "He completes me" or "She's so good for me." People in love utter these sentences wistfully.

At least they do for an average of five to nine years—because that's how long it takes the body to correct this chemical imbalance. It's as if the body maintenance person returns after an extended leave of absence and says, "Who the hell left the dopamine on?"—and then shuts it off. Now you look at your partner and say, "You've changed." No, they haven't changed; you're just not high anymore. You're off the drugs. You're clean; and without the chemicals, they ain't all that. The first thing you realize with this new perspective is that your intrinsic needs aren't being met. Romantics realize that they have not been appreciated for all the sacrifices they have made over the past seven years. They grow resentful. "Would it kill you to show me a little love?" they ask their Warrior spouses, seeking appreciation.

"I told you I loved you when we got married; I'll let you know if that changes," replies the Warrior. "We just talked about this issue six years ago. Stop nagging me." The Romantic grows clingier in hopes of getting more appreciation. The Warrior becomes more distant, looking for independence. Without the love drug to mask the symptoms, they suck the lifeblood right out of each other.

That's not to say that a Romantic and a Warrior can't have an enduring successful marriage. They absolutely *can*. The key is that they respect each other's style and provide for their respective intrinsic needs. Romantics who value the Warriors' direct, productive, and outcome-oriented approach and give their mates the independence to get results in their own way can be married to Warriors who appreciate the Romantics' sacrifices and peacemaking abilities and experience a wonderful relationship. It just takes some understanding of their diversity of contribution to the marriage. In fact, I think a strong argument can be made that having two diverse styles can be quite advantageous as a marriage evolves. It gives the couple a broader perspective on life issues.

This book focuses on four aspects of relationships: leadership, selling, service, and personal. What follows is an overview of how Romantics and Warriors approach each area.

ROMANTICS

Leading

Romantics are servant leaders. This means that they're most effective when they can remove emotional barriers to success and build happy, communicative teams. All Romantics want world peace and work tirelessly to make sure that their teams are emotionally secure. They focus on internal and external customer service and build strong relationships with their team members. Because they value communication, they hold frequent meetings and try to ensure everyone is in the loop. They are exceptional coaches and are quick to praise. They may struggle with delivering critical information and holding people accountable to a high standard because handling conflict can make them uncomfortable. They can also be susceptible to contributing to workplace drama when things are not going well, which can lead to reduced productivity. When working well, their teams are regarded for their high morale, low turnover, cohesiveness, and communication.

Selling

Romantics develop loyal customers by building relationships. They are likable, care about their clients, and work hard to get them a good deal. They may even sacrifice their own needs for the client's happiness. They take pride in the number of their customers who have become good friends. Because they care so deeply about their existing clients, they are often most comfortable working with them rather than seeking new opportunities. This is one of the challenges facing Romantic sales professionals. They can get so caught up in existing relationships that they don't have time to develop new ones. It is also important that they evaluate their existing relationships based on business potential—not just on the comfort with which they interact.

Serving

Romantics are very good at determining customers' emotional states. They can tell if a customer is not happy, even if the customer doesn't articulate it. They often possess the Servant's Heart—an almost innate desire to make others happy. Their easy smile and diplomacy makes them very effective at defusing problem customers, and although they may not always be patient, they can use their tact to mask frustrations. They are especially accomplished at active listening and making sure customers have fully vented their frustrations before beginning to fix the problem.

Personal

Romantics are often natural caregivers who want others to be happy. They show appreciation easily but may be a bit reticent to criticize or express frustrations. They often focus on fulfilling others' needs and may become somewhat resentful if that approach is not reciprocated. They enjoy creating deep, meaningful relationships with family and friends.

WARRIORS

Leading

Warriors are results-oriented leaders. They like to establish aggressive goals and then achieve them. They tend to be highly productive and value people who get things done. They are aware of the rules and may have even written them, but they do not let these rules interfere with the achievement of the goal. They reward people by leaving them alone and believe that "no news is good news." They often engage in a critical analysis of situations, looking for ways to enhance things. As a result, employees receive more criticism than praise and tend to see the Warrior as demanding or even angry. This can create morale concerns and increase turnover. When working well, their teams are noted for their high productivity, efficiency, and continual improvement.

Selling

Warriors are closers. They like to solve problems. They are most adept at analyzing a customer's need and offering solutions that will benefit the customer's situation. They are assertive negotiators and are very effective at coming to agreements that fiscally benefit their organization. Their efficient style ensures that they move quickly through the sales process to an outcome. They are also good at giving and receiving referrals and are often more comfortable in getting new business than maintaining existing relationships. Contrary to Romantics, Warriors can get so focused on hunting for new opportunities that they forget to farm the existing ones.

Serving

Warriors are good troubleshooters. They like to assess the situation quickly, determine the necessary resolution, and implement it. They recognize what needs to be done very quickly. They may not spend adequate time listening to the customer's frustration, simply because they have already figured out the problem and know how to solve it. Because they value time, they tend to work quickly to get the desired result.

Personal

Warriors are natural problem solvers. They value competence and allow others their space as long as they have proved to be good at what they do. Their strategic mind can make them excellent planners. They are comfortable with status because it reflects the fact that they are successful (winning). They appreciate confidence in others and respect those with whom they can have a direct conversation.

For you Warriors reading this book, here are the bullet points that describe each of these two styles:

Romantics	Warriors
• Trust their feelings (gut reaction) about situations and people • Sometimes value other's needs above their own • React strongly to emotion • Have a need to feel committed to another person, idea, or cause • Consider the impact of their actions on others' feelings • Value harmony among people with whom they interact • Show appreciation of others easily and respond to praise • Recognize the importance of tact and diplomacy • Have a strong desire to make a contribution • Are personable and talkative • May invest time in conversations unrelated to purpose • Loyal	• Trust logic and efficiency • Are competitive • Have a strong desire to improve • Are analytical • Value logic, justice, and fairness • Consider truth more important than tact • Believe feelings are valid only if they are logical • Are often seen as driven or extremely goal-oriented • Focus on enhancing rather than praising • Seem always to have a plan • Rarely act without a purpose • Get to the point quickly • May appear more irritated than they are, especially to Romantics • Talk fast

Romantics	Warriors
• Display an easy smile and laugh	• Want answers immediately
• Rarely criticize and express anger tactfully	• May expect things to be handled on their terms
• Are "honor bar" negotiators who use their likability to get the best deal	• Negotiate assertively
• Leadership style: Servant Leader	• Come across as very intelligent
• Selling style: Relationship Builder	• Not overly friendly, more intense
	• Leadership style: Results Leader
	• Selling style: Closer

There is much more to be learned about our Romantics and Warriors. But first there are three distinct types of each of these two styles. Those we will discover in Chapter 3. Later, we can explore how to best lead, sell to, provide service to, work with, and spend our personal time with each style. But before we do that, we still have two more styles to explore.

Chapter 2 Understanding Experts and Masterminds

Tried and True Contrasted with Possibilities

Now let's turn our attention to the other two interactive styles. Again, let me remind you that using these two styles to contrast each other doesn't mean that they are opposites, just very different. And that difference makes it easier to explain each style. If your lowest score is in column a, you are an Expert. Experts have sensitivity to facts as defined by situations, processes, approaches, and the like, with which they have had personal experience or that they can prove to be true. In general, Experts hate inaccuracies and work very hard to not make mistakes. I knew an Expert who made a mistake in 1996, but he is still researching it because he's pretty sure he was given the wrong information.

Experts aren't stubborn; they're *right!*

Experts like to know exactly what is expected of them. They thrive in structured environments that have clear instructions and well-defined policies and procedures in place. They are consistent, dependable, and reliable. They may not be tactful; it depends on the type of Expert. But they are patient. Patience, in the Expert world, means sustaining your focus on a task until you have accurately completed it. They often approach life like it was a flowchart, each step critical to ensuring a successful (accurate) outcome.

If your lowest score is in column c, you are a Mastermind. The Mastermind's motto is, "If it ain't broke, break it!" Masterminds are sensitive to the possibilities in their environment. They love to explore, experience new things, and think outside the box. In fact, they are often unaware there is a box. This fearlessness in the face of risk often makes them more entrepreneurial in their approach. They prefer more loosely defined situations and often thrive when allowed to experiment with their responsibilities or when they can work on special projects.

Masterminds tend to think more systemically. This makes their mind a little different than those of the other three styles. I like to imagine the other minds as working sequentially, one thing at a time. The Mastermind is working on everything at once, like a brainstorm. As a result, you may be having a conversation with a Mastermind and right in the middle of your discu—*squirrel!*

Masterminds are distracted. This behavior can be frustrating to the other styles who equate it to a lack of focus, but Masterminds don't really lack focus. The more accurate explanation would be they lack *interest*. You're boring! Since Masterminds have many other thoughts occurring in their heads, they can bounce to another when the current one becomes dull. Try waving a shiny thing to get them to return to your conversation. Kidding. (Kinda.)

(*Warning:* The following section represents the author's personal soapbox regarding the impact of technology on our education system.) As I mentioned earlier, experiences shape our schemas. The rapid introduction, adoption, and reengineering of technology has been occurring at a dizzying pace in recent years—and the speed is only increasing. Today, our children are using technology—sometimes far more effectively than adults—that didn't even exist in the last generation (or in some cases, in the last month!). In fact, technology is moving so quickly that the new software and devices being introduced annually radically change our lives. It stands to reason that this new existence, driven by technology, will create very different ways of thinking.

Let me give you an example. I have distinct memories of spending my summers as a kid with my best friend Dennis. His mother, Alice, was my caregiver while my parents were at work. Although it was great to hang out at my best friend's house all summer, being two 12-year-old boys, we would eventually run out of things to do. I remember entire days spent sitting on the steps of Dennis's house trying to come up with an idea to keep us entertained. These episodes could be painful, but when we finally came up with something, we were incredibly inspired. Over the years, we must have developed nearly a dozen different ways to reenact Major League Baseball games. Some were very simple, such as flipping a coin for each game on the schedule to see which teams would win the pennant. Others were very sophisticated, such as designing index cards for each player on each team with six columns and 11 rows full of options like outs, singles, doubles, triples, and home runs. Then we would play games with dice. We would even adjust the cards to better match the player's normal productivity. In hindsight, that's pretty intricate stuff for a couple of 12-year-olds.

We didn't have many options for entertainment. The television had only three channels, and daytime television in the 1970s was pretty lame for a preteen. We had no Internet, cell phone, laptop, tablet, iPod, or Kindle. We couldn't text, check

Facebook, or Skype anyone. We just sat there and thought of ways to entertain ourselves.

So when we went to school—which, make no mistake, we hated as much as kids today—we at least were wired for hours of boredom. We were prepared to invest in experiencing something unpleasant to get to what we liked.

Today, kids are experiencing a cornucopia of stimulation. Do you want to watch television? We have 1,000 channels. And you can talk to, call, text, chat with, or Skype a friend while you're doing it. Heck, in the six months between me writing this and the book being released, there may be 3D imaging or molecular transfer available. And, of course, there's the Internet. That information highway opens up as many possibilities as the imagination will allow.

In 2013, a young person need not delay gratification much beyond the occasional swirling cursor. It's a Mastermind's fantasy. Therefore, a significant number of kids are likely to develop a more Mastermind-oriented style.

Children who are used to constant and varied stimulation, custom-designed to their interests, would probably find our traditional school system to be a huge challenge. I mean, seriously, math for the next hour. Just math. For *an hour*. OMG! Worst. Day. Ever.

So what will happen? They bounce. They start thinking of things that are more interesting and stop paying attention to the class content. Remember, the first part of learning is the *absorb* activity; if you are not paying attention, you have effectively missed this step. You cannot connect or apply information that you never absorbed.

Given this set of circumstances, I think it is very reasonable to expect many otherwise bright kids to struggle in the traditional school system. Now, that doesn't mean they are gifted. I love that reasoning: "My Johnny struggles in school. It's because he's a genius, and the content isn't stimulating him." Sure, that could be true, but let's not get carried away. Johnny could be a perfectly normal, bright kid who just has trouble paying attention. That doesn't make him a genius. However, if Johnny starts getting bad grades, Johnny might start thinking he's stupid. *That* is the bigger issue.

Here's what I suggest. Don't get *too* hung up on the grades, particularly through high school. Parents and educators should focus more on self-efficacy. If our children maintain their confidence in themselves, then they will do just fine. Self-efficacy is a far more important factor in success and contentment than grade point average. Until we can install radical changes in our educational system, we will have to muddle through with our current process. I hope we don't inadvertently hamstring our youth while this transition occurs.

Now I'll step off my soapbox, so we can get back to our discussion of Experts and Masterminds. My primary interactive style is Romantic; my secondary is Warrior. You will soon learn what this combination means about how I communicate. Clearly, it means that I am generally very comfortable building rapport with Romantics and can adjust with minimal effort to interact successfully with Warriors. It also means I can find it more challenging to build a quick connection with and to communicate effectively with Experts and Masterminds.

My struggle to successfully adjust to the Expert style is not a new one for me. I remember spending summers working at my father's appliance/heating and air-conditioning store in a small Southern Illinois town called Greenup (population: 1,500). Dad was the primary source for home appliances, retrofitting old farmhouses with central heat and air conditioning, and for the occasional foray into illegal plumbing. My father was not a Romantic, and he didn't hire me because I was his son. My father was a Warrior, and I was employed because I was scrawny—a physicality perfectly designed for crawling under houses.

My father employed two other long-time contractors: Bob Haney and Richard "Dick" Lyons. Typically, Bob would do the majority of the appliance repair, and Dick would handle the majority of the heating and air-conditioning installations. Both Bob and Dick were Experts, both by interactive style and knowledge of their field. I worked with Dick most often.

Every time we would arrive at a home and begin the process of installing a new heating system, I would bound out of the truck and start unloading all the duct work and equipment. Dick would just shake his head and exhale an audible form of exasperation.

"Let's get the lay of the land before we start piling all this stuff around."

I remember thinking that Dick was just sandbagging. I was operating under the misguided notion that activity equaled productivity. But Dick, the Expert, realized that there was value to understanding exactly what you are about to get yourself into before you go off half-cocked. I still remember the many times I did something in the wrong order or completed a task in a somewhat sloppy way; Dick would look at my work and say, "What in Sam Hill is *that?*" At the time, it drove me crazy. As I learned more about interactive styles, I realized that for Dick Lyons, doing things right was much more important than doing things fast. (Sadly, I never figured out who or what Sam Hill was.)

It would still be many years before I would truly understand the mind of Experts and Masterminds. My teachers would be unlikely: a pair of yellow Labrador Retrievers named Martini and Rossi.

I learn from epiphanies. Maybe you learn this way, too. Sometimes an idea that I am familiar with just makes perfect sense to me for the very first time. It is like the concept has penetrated my intellect and my soul. Well, that may be a bit dramatic, but sometimes you just have that aha moment when something you knew in an academic way graduates to being something that becomes part of your behavior. My understanding of Experts and Masterminds was influenced by just such a moment shared with my canine buddies. Martini and Rossi are nearly identical to everyone but my wife, Lori, and me. Martini is slightly shapelier and better looking, a fact that has always created some resentment in Rossi. (For a full bio on the two, visit our website at www.theleadershipdifference.com.) When we adopted them, I knew right away that they would be true mountain dogs, able to roam around our property as sentinels and protectors. There's just one problem with that idea. There are a lot of things in the mountains that prize the nutritional value of two plump, domesticated yellow Labs. Clearly, they had to be contained within our yard—which posed a bit of a challenge. Putting a fence around our property was both expensive and aesthetically unattractive. Then I discovered a solution: the Invisible Fence.

I had never heard of this technology 11 years ago. For the unenlightened, the Invisible Fence is an ingenious invention involving three components: a buried wire (they now have wireless versions), a transmitter, and a special dog collar with a receiver. Pet owners simply bury the wire around the perimeter of their home and mark this area with white flags. The wire is then connected to the transmitter, which sends a signal to the dog's collar. As the dog wanders around the property, an audible warning sounds if the dog approaches the buried wire, marked by the white flags. This is designed to let the dog know that is as far as it is allowed to wander. Should the dog fail to heed the audible warning, the dog receives a "mild correction."

"Mild correction." That was the wording on both the website and the owner's manual.

The term *mild correction* is marketing genius when selling to a Romantic Warrior. *Mild* is very Romantic. *Correction* is very Warrior. My dogs can experience a mild correction in order to protect them. Brilliant! I bought it. A week later, I installed our new Invisible Fence. It took me only a couple of hours.

Now, I am one of those pet owners who refuse to subject my beloved Labs to anything that I have not *personally* experienced. So upon completing the installation, I walked into the house and announced to my lovely bride that I would now be experiencing the mild correction. Lori, who is infinitely smarter than me, grabbed a cup of coffee and walked out onto the deck to watch. (You can actually feel the love, can't you?) Anyway, I was committed to the entire experience, including the audible warning. Since I knew that dogs have greater hearing acuity than people, I had the dog collar up to my ear. Plus, I had imagined that the audible warning would be a soothing, slightly seductive female voice saying, "No, no, no; bad boy, bad boy." (Okay, so I travel a lot.)

As I walked toward the flags, I narrated my experience back to Lori. "Honey, I am practically on top of the flags, and I am not hearing any warning. Do you think I am too tall? Maybe I should get down on all fours . . . wait; I'm getting a series of beeps. I thin— . . . F#&%@CK!"

Mild correction, my butt! That thing altered the left hemisphere of my brain! I still drift to the right when I walk. That was *not* a mild correction. And I weigh about 185 pounds. The girls weigh maybe 80 . . . 85 . . . okay 90 pounds for Rossi. (She's big boned. She struggles with her weight.) Regardless, I am thinking that thing will *lobotomize* the dogs. I was mortified. My Romantic style was imploring me to not subject Martini and Rossi to this. My Warrior style was being rational. "They wouldn't sell a device that *harms* dogs, dude. You already bought it and installed it, and you don't have another solution. Use the fence."

A compromise was reached. I would thoroughly train Martini and Rossi to ensure that they would never experience the mild correction. Admittedly, I am not a very good dog trainer. If you spend any time with our pets, that fact is evident. My only memory of training dogs was the work of Ivan Pavlov relative to conditioned responses. Something about teaching the dog to salivate when it hears certain sounds by giving the dog a treat after making the sound. I knew Rossi was very food-motivated (see earlier comment regarding "struggles with her weight"), so I thought I could train her using Milk Bones.

I started thinking about Rossi's demeanor. She likes to be trained. She likes rules, policies, and tightly defined situations. She likes routines, arising at 6:30 AM and retiring to the garage at 7:00 PM every day. Her approach to most things is consistent and reliable. She does not like to take chances. Rossi is an Expert.

With a box of Milk Bones in one hand and Rossi on the leash in the other, we approached the white flags in the yard. Rossi would drift toward the flags to check them out and I would say, "No. Bad flag, bad flag! Have a Milk Bone." Now, Rossi doesn't speak English, so all she is getting is, "WAH. WAH WAH, WAH WAH. Milk Bone." "Milk Bone" she understands. Anyway, every time Rossi got near the flags, I said no and coaxed her back with the reward. By the eighth episode, Rossi would run back from the flags without even being coaxed, and as I gave her a Milk Bone, she would look at me with an expression that clearly communicated, "I *love* this game, Dad!"

By now, I had gotten cocky. Convinced that Rossi, was fully trained I gave her more space to explore the yard and avoid the flags. Unfortunately, I clearly didn't grasp the work of Ivan Pavlov. You see, conditioning requires two distinct components: rewards for desired behavior and penalties for noncompliance. I had worked only the first half of the equation. Now, after eight treats, Rossi was once again approaching the flags. I yelled, "No. Bad flags, bad flags. Milk Bone."

Rossi looked at me and thought, "Meh, I've had eight Milk Bones. I wonder what I get if I go beyond the flags; maybe a pound of beef!" Rossi kept going. And then I saw her head tilt, and I knew she was receiving the audible warning. A quick calculation of time and distance compared to my foot speed and I realized that I could not intervene.

I would not consider Rossi to be a particularly athletic dog, but on this occasion she exhibited what NBA scouts would refer to as major ups. Her vertical leap was at least 4 feet high, and what made it even more impressive was that I saw no evidence that she used any muscles to achieve it. She used only the power of her paws. Once mid-air, she violated several of Newton's theories by willing herself vertically toward the house while emitting a sound that I would describe as part bark, part yelp, and part . . . umm . . . canine profanity—clearly directed at me. That dog sprinted back in the house like she was shot out of a cannon—and for the next three days, she peed on our welcome mat. Yep. I would let her out, and she would squat immediately outside the door, all the time looking around as if there was evilness lingering in the yard.

Today, some 11 years later, that dog walks the perimeter of our yard. Her collar doesn't even work. She follows the rules, avoids the long-gone flags and stays true to her training. If Lori and I decided to move, Rossi would remain, knowing the penalty for noncompliance. She takes her training seriously and does not want to disappoint those who have entrusted her with the responsibility of protecting the house from those flags. Rossi is an Expert.

However, I still had one more dog to train. Martini loves to explore. She has that sparkle in her eye that is simultaneously charming and mischievous. She disappears for long periods of time while on hikes, returning with something dead in her mouth and a prance that clearly states, "Hey, Dad, you won't believe the cool thing I found." She is easily distracted and cheerfully noncompliant. Martini was going to be deep fried to a crackly crunch by the Invisible Fence, and I wanted no part of it.

I put the collar on Martini, opened the door, and said, "Knock yourself out, baby doll."

Well, apparently Martini had talked to Rossi. That makes perfect sense. If something traumatic has happened to your sister, you are bound to discuss it in the crate. I can only imagine a shaken Rossi coming back after her experience with the bad flags and, when asked by Martini what the heck happened, saying, "I don't know, but if you hear a series of beeps, get the hell out of Dodge!" The first clue that Rossi had shared her experience with Martini was in the demeanor that Martini displayed when I let her out of the house. She flew out the house, barking ferociously, and ran hell-bent for the flags. I cringed, realizing that Martini was about to exact her revenge on the attackers, unaware of the consequences. As she bound toward the flags I prepared for the inevitable. As she neared the closest flag, I saw her head tilt and I knew she was receiving the audible warning.

Then something remarkable happened.

She stopped.

She stopped and backed away from the flag. Just as her sister warned her, the series of beeps were the harbinger of the flag's bite. Martini now eyed the flags, her Mastermind brain trying to get her head around the concept. She began to stalk the flag. Each time she got close, she would tilt her head and back away. But each time she would back away less. After about 15 minutes of this process, Martini had localized the electronic field of the Invisible Fence to a matter of inches. There she was, in the play posture—front legs extended fully, rear end up in the air, rocking front to back. I watched as Martini continued this approach for several more minutes, rocking back and forth, back and forth, until finally . . . she wore the battery out in her collar. No beeps. She attacked. She pulled every flag out of ground, shook it, and cast it aside. She then looked back at me as if to say, "Oh snap— were you trying to contain me? Well, how do you like me now?"

To this day, Martini's collar battery lasts about two weeks. She spends much of her day checking to see if it still beeps. We don't worry about her escaping, though—because every time she does manage to break the perimeter, Rossi—the Expert—starts barking. "She can't do that! She's outside the flags! Dad! *Dad!*"

This same dynamic happens every day in the corporate world: A Mastermind circumvents the rules only to have an Expert chasten him or her about compliance.

And so it was how two yellow Labs taught this Romantic Warrior the fundamentals of the Expert and the Mastermind styles.

Experts tend be very detailed and thorough when approaching any project, whereas Masterminds are content to outline the big picture. It's like comparing a procedure to a guideline, a policy to a philosophy. If you are not sure if someone is an Expert, ask the person for directions.

"Hey, Bob, do you know where the chiropractor is on Oak Street?"

Bob (Expert): "Hmmm, the chiropractor on Oak Street. That's got to be the Spinal Institute. Hmm . . . yes . . . yes, I do. Where are you parked?"

"Umm . . . in the parking lot."

"The one on the left side of the building or the one on the right?"

"Left."

"Okay, good. There's only one way out of that lot. You got to go right out of the lot on Main. You will immediately come to a stoplight, that's Hickory Street."

"What do I do there?"

"Nothing. Just keep going. You will go two more blocks until you get to the second light. That's Walnut Street. Now, there's no street sign at that intersection. I noticed that just the other day. I don't know if someone hit it or if they are changing the signs and haven't put up the new sign, but there is no indication that is Walnut. But it is—and let me tell you how I know that. I actually grew up seven blocks south of that intersection, and in the summer, I used to ride my bike up that that same intersection you will be at, Main and Walnut. There was a family grocery store there named Elmer's Grocery. They carried Yoo-Hoo Chocolate Soda. Do they still make that? Man, I used to love that stuff as a kid. I need to Google that when I get home. Now, don't look for that store; it's gone. Elmer died. Gosh, he's been dead for more than 20 years. Well, you know what; I'll tell you exactly when he died: 1986. And I'll tell you how I know that. Elmer was from Brooklyn, and he was the only New York Mets fan I ever met around here. In 1986, the Mets won the World Series and Elmer died about a month later. I always thought he just hung around long enough to see his beloved team win that series. They tore down that store within a year of his passing. I guess the family didn't have any interest in competing with those big grocery chains."

"Uh, Bob, what do I do at Walnut?"

"Oh, nothing. Just keep going down Main . . ."

You can learn a lot about interactive style by watching how people react to Bob's Expert directions. If Bob is talking to another Expert, that person finds all this extraneous information very interesting. The other Expert will happily discuss the 1986 World Series, the demise of small businesses, and the relative merits of Yoo-Hoo Chocolate Soda. That's a great exchange for Experts.

If Bob is talking to a Romantic, the Romantic nods and encourages Bob with responses such as, "Well, at least he got to see his team win" and "I really appreciate these detailed directions." At least that's what Romantics *say*. They are *thinking*, "Note to self: *Never* ask Bob for directions again. Dear Lord. Bless his heart. Sweet man, but *wow* is he wordy." The Romantic endures the conversation because Bob is trying to provide help and it would be rude to stop him.

The Mastermind wouldn't even ask for directions in the first place; the journey is the fun part. The Mastermind would download a couple of apps, turn on her GPS device, and head out. "It's New York City. How hard can it be?" An hour later the Mastermind returns and the Romantic might ask, "How was your chiropractic appointment?" "Dang it!" exclaims the Mastermind. "Chiropractor. That's right. Oh well, check out my manicure!"

It's the Warrior who has a cerebral hemorrhage talking to Bob. The Warrior's idea of directions are something like, "Take a right out of the lot, go five blocks, turn left, and you will see it on the right just a couple of blocks up." A 20-second conversation, tops. No Hickory Street. No Walnut Street. *Certainly* no memories of Elmer's Grocery, the 1986 World Series, or Yoo-Hoo Chocolate Sodas. "For the love of God, Bob, get a life. I'm going on MapQuest."

Experts tend to avoid or minimize risk, whereas Masterminds embrace it. Experts learn by research and want to avoid chaos, whereas Masterminds often learn by trial and error and are comfortable in—even relish—chaos. Mistakes are like Scud missiles for the Expert: to be avoided at all costs. Should someone make a mistake, you fling it back. Masterminds are Scud-proof. When a Mastermind makes a mistake, the Expert says, "Well, you screwed that up," to which the Mastermind responds, "Yep, but I learned a ton."

Experts' intrinsic need is *security*. They like things to be reliable and consistent and revel in the feeling that things are as they should be. Masterminds' intrinsic need is *excitement*. They love new, different, and customized experiences. I always imagine an Expert and Mastermind marrying and deciding on the summer vacation. The Expert wants to buy a condo at her favorite getaway so they can enjoy every vacation in their leisure home away from home. The Mastermind thinks, "Yeah, that sounds amazing. Let's spend every future vacation at the same place. Goodness knows there is *nowhere else on the planet I want to see.*" It makes perfect sense that the two would fall in love—much like the Romantic and the Warrior. One provides stability and reliability; the other, innovation and experimentation. Of course, if they don't learn to respect that, the Mastermind may view the Expert as boring and the Expert may view the Mastermind as exhausting.

Just as we did with Romantics and Warriors, let's examine how Experts and Masterminds approach leading, selling, serving, and personal relationships.

EXPERTS

Leading

Experts are thought leaders. They often have more technical knowledge than any other member of their team. They are well versed in the policies, procedures, practices, and processes that affect the workplace. They value accuracy and operate with a similar philosophy as a Lean Six Sigma practitioner. They prefer refining over reinventing. They can be rigid and historically based, which can lead to challenges during change initiatives. When working well, the Expert-led team produces high-quality outputs that are compliant with all regulations and requirements.

Selling

Experts sell with knowledge. They take great pride in learning everything about their products and services. There is not a question that they cannot answer. Their guidance is accurate, and they often are very thorough in training their customers about the features and benefits of their offerings. They are organized in their approach and often use a formal system for identifying opportunities, documenting progress, and following up with clients. They may struggle with new products and services until they feel knowledgeable enough to represent them and they may become a bit too feature-driven when selling because of their depth of familiarity.

Serving

Experts use their thorough knowledge of their services and the system to provide their clients with exactly what they were promised. They take their responsibilities seriously and know how to do their job. They approach each customer the same way: with the commitment to deliver a quality experience based on their knowledge and training.

Personal

Experts value security and prefer for things to happen in a predictable way. They are reassured by familiarity. Things that they have personally experienced—that they have seen, heard, smelled, tasted, or touched—are the most appealing to them. History is the best predictor of the future.

MASTERMINDS

Leading

Masterminds are visionary leaders. They are comfortable embracing cutting-edge ideas and experiencing the risk associated with being an early adopter. They are entrepreneurial and fearless in taking chances. They like to experiment and engage in new and different ways of thinking. They are capable of generating very innovative ideas and approaches. Their high risk tolerance can lead to mistakes and create some chaos. They also have a tendency to focus more on the vision than the execution, which can lead to a lack of details and unclear strategies. When working well, the Mastermind-led team is enthusiastic, creative, energized, and inspired to introduce new and different products/services.

Selling

Masterminds sell with vision and enthusiasm. They get excited about the possibilities and can instill in your mind an image of a wondrous and desirable future state that does not exist today. They embrace trends and encourage others to be early adopters, too. They are comfortable expanding relationships beyond the customer's stated needs and love to explore the global view versus the narrow view. It is this passion for possibilities that can lead them to introduce ideas at the expense of closing the original sale. They benefit by being careful not to complicate a transaction with options before securing a commitment on the fundamental deal.

Serving

Masterminds offer creative solutions. They are very comfortable, even excited by, working with exceptional scenarios. They will circumnavigate the rules if necessary to achieve a mutually acceptable resolution. Because they think like an entrepreneur, they are comfortable in creating precedence where no one else has ventured to go.

Personal

Boredom is the Mastermind's number one enemy. Masterminds crave new and different experiences and are often quite charming and energetic. They will remain engaged and excited in a relationship that offers a continually stimulating environment of options, uniqueness, and enthusiasm.

Again, as a public service to the Warriors reading this book, here are some bullet points about both the Experts and Masterminds:

Experts	Masterminds
• Trust what is certain and concrete	• Trust inspiration and inference
• Value realism and common sense	• Value imagination and innovation
• Like to apply and hone established skills	• Like to learn new skills; become bored with things already mastered
• Tend to be specific and literal	• Often use metaphors to explain their ideas
• Give detailed instructions	• Present information in large chunks or in a roundabout manner
• Present information in a step-by-step manner	
• Are focused on the present	

(*continued*)

(*continued*)

Experts	Masterminds
• Have great respect for the rules	• Tend to be impractical dreamers
• Value consistency and reliability	• Can appear to be disorganized and absentminded
• Respond best to a salesperson or customer service provider who is knowledgeable	• Seek change, take risks, and are comfortable in chaos
• Often have great depth of knowledge about the process	• Respond to a salesperson or servicer who is flexible and innovative
• If lacking depth of knowledge, may want to obtain it from you	• May go off on tangents during conversations
• Very specific with their questions and requests	• Will challenge you to provide options or exceptions
• Disappointed if things don't go exactly as they were told	• Often very charming and enthusiastic
• May appear stubborn on small issues	• May forget some of the content of previous discussions
• Complete assignments on time and are detailed	• Often use language like "What if" or "Would it be possible"
• Like appointments for callbacks and upcoming interactions	• Are less specific and more general in their questions and expectations
• Leadership style: Thought Leader	• Leadership style: Visionary Leader
• Selling style: Subject Matter Expert	• Selling style: Innovative Solutions

Now that we have addressed the four interactive styles in general terms, it is time to explore the various primary and secondary combinations that form your Hollywood movie character. Get your assessments ready—because now the *real* fun begins!

Chapter 3 The 12 Interactive Combinations—Hollywood Style!

THE BEST FRIEND

- Lowest score in column b
- Next lowest score in column a
- Romantic/Expert
- In a nutshell: "If you need a hug and a shoulder to cry on, the Best Friend is your person."

I always begin with this combination during my seminars. I have them stand up and pronounce them to be "the nicest people in the room." Best Friends always have their "spoons" ready to help others empty the crap out of their CTL container. They are the master counselors, the best at navigating the venting process. If you are having trouble and need someone to talk to, there is no better person than the Best Friend.

Best Friends are also steady, dependable contributors. They rarely make mistakes and work very well within a structured environment. They are comfortable with policies and procedures and respect the organization's processes and hierarchy.

Here are a few words that would describe the Best Friend:

- Compassionate
- Caring
- Empathetic
- Reliable
- Consistent
- Trustworthy
- Patient
- Tactful
- Accurate
- Steady
- Methodical
- Thorough

Is it any wonder that they are the Best Friend? Now, they *do* have their vulnerabilities. First, they can be a little stubborn. Their way of doing things minimizes mistakes, so they are generally surprised when someone tells them they're inaccurate. Here is a typical conversation that may ensue when someone accuses a Best Friend of a mistake.

Supervisor: Hey, Betty, you screwed up your paperwork.

Betty (Best Friend): What? I am so sorry! What did I do?

Supervisor: This number is wrong. I'm not sure where you got that figure, but it is not accurate.

Betty: Really? Huh. Wow. Well, I do apologize. I am pretty sure that was what I was told to put there.

Supervisor: Well, I'm just saying it's wrong.

Betty: Okay. Again, I apologize. I hope I didn't cause any problems. I could have sworn that was how I was trained. *One hour later . . .*

Betty *(walks into the supervisor's office)*: I don't know if you have seen this memo, but the reason I completed the paperwork that way was based on this.

The mistake isn't sticking.

Best Friends are the protectors of their flocks. They are like a shepherd, diligently herding their sheep safely to their destination. They carry a staff, but it is not for battling the wolves. The staff is for gently nudging the sheep away from danger. Best Friends often are a little more critical and demanding of those whom they love and feel responsible for because they are trying to keep them *safe*.

As leaders, Best Friends provide a steadying influence. They have almost a parental relationship with their team. They create well-defined roles and responsibilities. They often know a great deal about the line-level job and may have once done it for a living. They enforce procedures and run a tight ship when it comes to compliance. They spend ample time in coaching and counseling. They may struggle a bit with conflict and have a tendency to avoid uncomfortable conversations. They don't necessary pursue or even enjoy change initiatives; however, they are very important to this effort because they can challenge the effectiveness of new approaches and patiently train staff members on new systems and processes. Best Friend leaders often achieve high levels of morale, good communication, few mistakes, and low turnover. They create a *family* within their teams.

As sales professionals, Best Friends are the consummate relationship builders. They diligently devote themselves to understanding their products and services and work hard to develop meaningful, long-term relationships with clients built on friendship, trust, and reliability. Their credibility on both a personal and a professional level makes them appealing to people who enjoy working with a knowledgeable friend. Their customers are loyal and depend on them for accurate, thoughtful advice. However, they may struggle when dealing with customer objections because the dynamic can feel antagonistic. They also may not close aggressively, because applying pressure on the customer may feel slightly confrontational. Keep in mind that people can develop skills in an area that may not be natural for them based on their style. Given that, there is no reason to believe that Best Friends can't learn to handle closing and objections quite well.

As service providers, Best Friends want to take care of you. They want to make sure that you are happy and that you received accurate information. They keep their promises and feel emotionally vested in your satisfaction. They will be very thorough in ensuring that your experience meets your expectations. They will take any mistake very seriously and apologize profusely. Many Best Friends have made friends with their customers.

Best Friends are often the team members to whom others vent. They generally have a keen awareness of the organization's morale. They are reliable performers who approach their jobs with steadiness, knowledge, and caution. Although they're good team players, they may shy away from confronting others. They may also become a bit passive-aggressive if they don't think their leader values them. They work best in environments that offer abundant praise, are well structured, and have clear direction and expectations.

Hollywood casts the Best Friend in a supporting role most often. Every romantic comedy has a main character whose life is a bit chaotic and whose adventures become the plot development. By the main character's side is his or her trusted, reliable Best Friend. This person is commonly more settled down, often married, and tries to offer some advice and stability to the main character. That is the role of the Best Friend, to maintain or restore the calm during chaos. Some iconic Best Friends in Hollywood: Mary Tyler Moore, Rachel in *Friends*, and almost any role featuring John Goodman.

Here's a quick reference guide for the Best Friend.

Role	Qualities
Leadership	• Quick to praise • Great coach • May be slow to criticize • Adept at allowing others to vent • Complies with rules • Consistent • Makes few mistakes • May be slow to change • Very aware of employee morale • Loyal to the team and the organization
Sales Professional	• Creates long-term relationships • Builds existing customer business • Has great knowledge of the product • May struggle with closing • May struggle with objections • Will be compliant with paperwork and process requirements
Service Provider	• Will provide accurate information to customers • Empathizes with the customer's situation • Listens actively • May be overly influenced by emotional issues • May lack creativity in resolving customer needs • Is polite and cordial to customers • Gets to know customers personally

THE LOVE INTEREST

- Lowest score in column b
- Next lowest score in column c
- Romantic/Mastermind
- In a nutshell: "Ready to let your hair down and have some fun? Call the Love Interest."

If the Best Friend is the nicest person in the room, then the Love Interest is the most charming. I have to admit that I am a little biased on this particular pattern, and not because it's mine—it is my wife's. It is also a common pattern among my friends. Love Interests' emotional sensitivity combined with their enthusiasm for new things and possibilities just gives them a certain *je ne sais quoi.*

Love Interests are like the world's public relations/marketing people, running around spreading joy and optimism. They are the people who make the rounds on Monday morning, checking on everyone, finding out how their weekends went. They lift morale by sharing good cheer and enthusiasm. Warriors watch Love Interests' tireless efforts to lift spirits and wonder, "Do they *do* anything here, or do they just talk to people all day?" Love Interests respond, "Is your underwear too tight? Lighten up. You're the buzzkill around here and the reason I need to do this!"

Here are a few words that describe Love Interests. (Because they are a fellow Romantic to the Best Friend, you will notice some similarities.)

- Kind
- Enthusiastic
- Diplomatic
- Tactful
- Bubbly

- Gregarious
- Friendly
- Eager
- Optimistic
- Flexible
- Charming

If you want to have fun, hang out with a Love Interest. Love Interests are very supportive of other people's dreams and tolerate enough risk to take chances on something new and different. They strive for world peace by focusing on a better future, and their optimism is infectious. Although they may not have a clear plan or details, they are confident that things will work out just fine.

My wife, Lori (a Love Interest), is the reason I started the Leadership Difference in 1995. After years of agonizing over the decision, it was this conversation that compelled me to start my new journey:

Dave: I would *so* like to just leave the corporate world and do my own thing. I want to train people on leadership and other skills without the restriction of the corporate structure.

Lori: Then do it.

Dave: But what if I fail? What if it doesn't work?

Lori: What would happen if you fail?

Dave: I would have to go back to a conventional job and probably be just as unhappy as I am now.

Lori: So you are unhappy in a conventional job now. If you take the chance to start your own company, you'll either be happy and successful—or have to return to the current state you are in. It sounds to me like there's no risk at all. If it works, you have more than you have today; if it fails, your situation hasn't changed. What's to lose?

(Crickets.)

Dave: Good point.

As a leader, the Love Interest is a cheerleader. Love Interests create environments that are fun and full of energy. They are attentive to the team's morale and quick to praise individuals. They introduce new and different ideas to maintain the staff's excitement. They are great coaches but may struggle with providing critical feedback because they typically dislike conflict or confrontation. They are loyal to both the team and the organization at large. Generally, they create environments that are full of appreciation, new ideas, and excitement, and they are natural team builders.

As sales professionals, Love Interests build relationships with their charms. They are enthusiastic about their organization's products/services and are eager to understand their customer's needs so that they can make their future better. They find creative ways to help others and are excellent at entertaining. They invest heavily in getting to know their customers as people, particularly during the beginning of the sales process.

As service providers, Love Interests are upbeat and energetic, particularly when the service is being well received by the customer. They are also adept at finding inventive solutions to the customer's concerns. However, repeated exposure to negative customer feedback can reduce their motivation. They work best with customers who are also positive and enthusiastic. When in this situation, Love Interest are excellent representatives of the organization.

As team members, Love Interests are fun to be around, people with whom other team members enjoy working. They thrive in emotionally positive environments that offer new and exciting opportunities. They will be demotivated by monotonous and repetitive work and by rigid or negative people. They also tend to be very social and enjoy coordinating activities that gather the group together.

Hollywood adores the Love Interest. Every romantic comedy is built on at least one. Think about the standard rom-com: There is always a main character who is very lovable but whose life is slightly chaotic. This character remains optimistic that good things are to come, but the world keeps throwing barriers in the way. But if the Love Interest perseveres with charm and enthusiasm, eventually, his or her dreams come true. For women, there is a long and stellar list of actresses who have portrayed the Love Interest—from Julia Roberts in *Pretty Woman* and Meg Ryan in *When Harry Met Sally* all the way through today's female leads like Anne Hathaway and Drew Barrymore. For men, the iconic Love Interest of the early twenty-first century was Hugh Grant. You don't go to a Hugh Grant movie to see him pop a cap in someone's butt. Hugh is a lover. Other actors who have portrayed the Love Interest role are Hugh Jackman (what's with the Hugh connection?) and Ryan Reynolds. Cary Grant and Jimmy Stewart are among the classic actors who excelled in the role. *It's a Wonderful Life* is the quintessential Love Interest movie.

Role	Qualities
Leadership	• Quick to praise
	• Lobbies for others
	• Reluctant to criticize
	• Introduces fun activities and element in workplace
	• Flexible
	• Promotes high morale
	• Takes on new projects with enthusiasm
	• Communicates positive messages about change
	• May avoid conflict with others
	• Promotes the company's products and/or services
Sales Professional	• Establishes new relationships
	• Has many loyal customers

(*continued*)

(*continued*)

Role	Qualities
	• Very enthusiastic about products and services
	• May struggle with closing and dealing with objections
	• Great networker
	• May not be adept at the structure and paperwork
Service Provider	• Excellent at turning around unhappy customers
	• Empathizes with the customer's situation
	• Listens actively
	• May be overly influenced by emotional issues
	• Finds creative ways to satisfy customer demands
	• May be susceptible to burn out if they must continually deal with negative customers
	• Gets to know their customers personally
Team Member	• Well liked by others
	• Enthusiastic
	• Flexible with new assignment; actually enjoys the variety
	• Wants to make their boss happy
	• May struggle with jobs that are dull, repetitive, or negative
	• Responds to the appreciation of the leader and the opportunity to be involved in fun assignments
	• Very aware of the morale of colleagues

THE CRUSADER

- Lowest score in column b
- Next lowest score in column d
- Romantic/Warrior
- In a nutshell: "The self-sacrificing hero accepting responsibility for others and the cause."

As discussed previously, all Romantics want world peace. They work hard to make sure everyone is happy and getting along. To review: Best Friends use security and counseling to achieve world peace. They provide compassionate stability that comforts those around them. Love Interests use joy and optimism to achieve world peace. They provide enthusiasm and fun to ensure that the future is even better than the present. And Crusaders get world peace by killing.

However, they often don't *want* to do it. "Who do I have to kill to make you happy?" wonder the Crusaders. They take no joy from the kill and would prefer to find alternative solutions to the barriers to world peace, but when forced into action to resolve an issue, they kill. This can come as quite a surprise to their fellow Romantics, because many of their colleagues had no idea the Crusader was armed. Their weapons are concealed, and their skills to wield them are rarely displayed. But you can rest assured, the Crusader is packin'.

Here are a few words that would describe Crusaders:

- Fiercely loyal
- Committed
- Empathetic
- Caring
- Assertive
- Tactful, but not patient
- Strategic

- Competitive
- Conflicted (win or be liked?)
- Productive
- Responsible
- Solution-focused

Crusaders walk a challenging line between wanting to be liked and wanting to win. This can cause them some significant stress and often leads them to take on more than their share of responsibility. They are comfortable pushing the process along toward a result but will also monitor the team's feelings carefully while progressing toward that goal. Pity the poor malcontent that either upsets the people or inhibits the results. Imagine the workplace being more like a scene from *Braveheart*.

Crusader: Come on, everyone. Let's move together toward our goal.

The team: We are trying, but Mark is impeding our progress. He does not believe in our crusade.

Crusader *(clearly concerned)*: What? That's crazy. Mark must not understand our crusade. Let me talk to Mark.

Crusader: Mark? Hey man, listen. I'm getting some feedback from my team that you don't support our crusade. Clearly, you must not understand it, or you would surely join us.

Mark: No, I understand it. I think it's stupid.

Crusader: Stupid! Wow. Um . . . okay, well, perhaps you could just step aside. You see, you are upsetting my people.

Mark *(continuing to impede the team's progress)*: I won't step aside, because I think this is the wrong thing to do. Furthermore, I think we should put a sto—

(Crusader thrusts a sword into Mark's torso.)

Crusader: I *really* wish you had just stepped aside, Mark. Do you think I like doing that? I hate using my sword. Come on, everyone, let's keep going. Watch out for Mark. *(Steps over Mark's body.)*

What really bothers the Crusader is that now his or her own team is a bit upset. "I can't believe you killed Mark!" they exclaim.

"Well, you were all complaining about him. I had to do *something!*" the Crusader reasons.

Crusaders fight for their teams' cause, which is generally some identified result that will have a positive impact on the people to whom they feel an alliance. Crusaders' internal conflict comes from maintaining the emotional contentment of those around them while simultaneously pursuing the desired outcome.

As leaders, Crusaders can be very protective of their people. They will appreciate their accomplishments while also expecting them to contribute to achieving the desired goal. They will give measured criticism, trying to ensure that they get the results they need without creating any ill will among the team members. They often take on additional responsibility. They like metrics on important processes and approach meetings with a clear agenda for enhancing the team's productivity while also keeping morale high. They give their team members' independence, particularly those who are performing well. Although they do not enjoy conflict, they will engage in counseling when it is clear that a person is not willing or able to contribute to the cause.

As sales professionals, Crusaders take the consummate consultative approach. They listen to their clients' needs and develop clear strategies for helping them with their challenges. Crusaders use both relationship building and logic to develop a strategy that benefits both parties, and they will sacrifice their own needs if necessary to make a deal work. They are comfortable finding new clients, but truly enjoy the satisfaction of solving existing clients' new problems.

As service providers, Crusaders work hard to make others happy. They know how to get results by working both inside the system or, if necessary, taking some shortcuts. They are good in the service recovery role because they are excellent troubleshooters. They may even be more committed to the customer than to their own company if they believe that the customer was treated wrongly or did not receive what was promised.

As team members, Crusaders are generally very productive members of the team. They get things done. They are comfortable working with others but may prefer to work independently the majority of the time. They are diplomatic but also eager to see things improve. This combination may make them the most likely to speak out against policies or actions that they think are wrong for the people. In this way, they can become the very malcontent that they often kill. (See the earlier Mark story.)

Hollywood casts the Crusader in the hero role. The Crusader is often viewed as a selfless fighter fighting for an underdog cause. For years, Hollywood called one person when they needed a leading man to play the role of the Crusader: Mel Gibson. Plot: He's happy and content and living in the Outback of Australia. They kill his wife. Now, he's *Mad Max*. Plot: He's happy and content and living in New England. They kill his son. Now, he's *The Patriot*. Plot: He's happy and content. They kill his wife *and* take his land. Now, he's *Braveheart*. He is the Crusader in each movie; he just wears different period costumes. Of course, Mel has displayed some unfortunate personal characteristics that have eroded his box office appeal since his heyday. Enter Gerard Butler in *300*. "We are Sparta!" For the women, Jennifer Lawrence in *The Hunger Games* is a great example of the Crusader.

Here's a quick reference guide for the Crusader:

Role	Qualities
Leadership	• Provides a mix of praise and carefully worded criticism • Very loyal to the cause (his or her team, the organization, the customer) • Diplomatic

Role	Qualities
	• Has a slight intensity that is masked with tact
	• Likes metrics that measure success
	• Less rule-bound, more goal-oriented
	• Organizes meetings around outcomes
	• Analytical but gives morale issues priority
	• Grows more tense when results are not achieved
	• Eager for more responsibility
Sales Professional	• Builds relationships with productive clients
	• Exceptional consultative salesperson
	• Sees a clear strategy to achieving the desired outcome
	• Negotiates win-win outcomes
	• May take the outcome personally
	• Has a tendency to overextend himself or herself to please the client or company
Service Provider	• Identifies needs and problems quickly
	• Is motivated by resolving barriers
	• Gets results quickly
	• Works hard for customers that have been poorly treated
	• Knows ways around the process to achieve solutions
	• Engages in some relationship building and then quickly transitions to the business purpose of transaction
	• Is sometimes asked for by name by repeat customers

(continued)

(continued)

Role	Qualities
Team Member	• Likable but may prefer to work independent of others • Gets things done • Likes to be appreciated and also left alone by his or her leader • Good troubleshooter • Likes new assignments if a clear expected outcome has been identified • May question direction not agreed with • Strives to be considered the best • Tactful with coworkers but interested in working directly only with the ones who are competent and have shared goals

THE HIRED GUN

- Lowest score in column d
- Next lowest score in column b
- Warrior/Romantic
- In a nutshell: "If you want something done without creating hard feelings, give it to the Hired Gun."

If the Crusader kills for a cause, then the Hired Gun kills for the contract. Hired Guns are charismatic competitors, able to win battles without making enemies. Hired Guns' confidence, diplomacy, and ability to get a desired outcome without creating ill will makes them among the most effective of negotiators. They have a natural swagger and often display signs of status with their personal style or in the products they purchase (cars, homes, jewelry, etc.). They are the smiling Warrior and can be described with words such as:

- Confident
- Competitive
- Assertive
- Diplomatic
- Personable
- Charismatic
- Results-oriented
- Productive
- Savvy negotiator
- Politically adept
- Suave
- Self-possessed

As implied in the name, Hired Guns get paid. One of the best cinematic representations of this style is the legendary character of James Bond. Bond is rarely seen in meetings or conference calls; he receives his mission and is left alone to execute as he sees fit. His swagger is evident, yet he is seemingly well liked by even his enemies. In fact, his nemesis works very hard to find a creative way to kill Bond, something befitting his stature. As a show of respect, the archenemy then must spend a great deal of time explaining how and why he will kill 007. By the time the villain has communicated his intentions to James, Bond has managed to escape.

Even though Hired Guns may operate outside the rules, they are generally well liked by their peers. They get things done. They have an easy smile. They work hard to realize the goal they are given, and they expect to be paid in return. Again, think about James Bond. He has been placed in harm's way, but in the meantime, he is drinking a martini while wearing an Armani tuxedo and sleeping with Jinx Johnson (played by Halle Berry). He is getting compensated. It's a good gig.

The combination of swagger, competitiveness, and charm can push Hired Guns to the brink of cocky. Their dual ability to close aggressively and build a relationship makes them innate salespersons. This is their unique value. They are the kind of people who invite you to play golf, challenge you with a friendly wager on every hole, and beat you soundly—and yet you still want to play another round with them next week.

As leaders, Hired Guns inspire others to achieve their goals through a combination of appreciation and freedom. They build strong relationships with their staff, particularly those who perform the best. They respect those who get results. They are comfortable with all forms of feedback and will not suffer fools silently, but rather they will engage them in direct counseling. They will allow some latitude on how followers obtain results, especially the ones who have an established record of achieving goals.

Hired Guns are natural sales professionals. They build relationships strategically, investing enough time in getting to know their clients while adeptly transitioning to the selling process. Typically, they are both good closers and adept negotiators. They may struggle with highly technical products or processes but will likely develop other resources within the organization to complement them. They can nimbly handle objections without creating an antagonistic relationship with their customer.

As service providers, Hired Guns are excellent troubleshooters who can quickly surmise the nature of the problem and solve it. They actively listen to customers' situations, always with an ear for the key factors that will determine the strategy for addressing their concerns. Hired Guns may lose interest in what they consider unnecessary details or unrelated tangents, but they maintain their service-oriented demeanor.

Hired Guns are well-liked team members but prefer to work independently of others. This is especially true when they are compensated directly for their efforts. They are most motivated by situations that allow them to get the desired result without too much oversight. They exhibit sufficient tact and diplomacy to minimize any negative morale implications that can arise from their occasional rule transgressions.

Action movies are the domain of Hired Guns. Like James Bond, Hired Guns are asked to achieve a mission and do so with both efficiency and style. They ooze a sort of sophistication even as they are evading an assassin. This grace under fire helps them maintain the foundation of their relationships with others, even as they compete with them. It is that delicate balance that is the genius of the Hired Gun. Some iconic Hired Guns in Hollywood include Sean Connery, Daniel Craig, Bruce Willis, Dwayne "The Rock" Johnson, Demi Moore, Angelina Jolie, Kathleen Turner, Jennifer Garner, and Jennifer Lawrence's Katniss Everdeen in *The Hunger Games*. My personal favorite iconic Hired Gun is Robert Redford's Butch Cassidy from the movie *Butch Cassidy and the Sundance Kid*.

Here's a quick reference guide for the Hired Gun:

Role	Qualities
Leadership	• Provides both praise and independence
	• Coaches and counsels equally
	• May work outside the rules on occasion
	• Values both results and relationships
	• Politically adept
	• Negotiates assertively
	• Values outcomes more than compliance
	• Good communicator of strategies
	• Interested in morale but not necessarily influenced by it
	• Likes incentives that drive performance
Sales Professional	• Consultative approach
	• Savvy closer and negotiator

(*continued*)

(continued)

Role	Qualities
	• Navigates organizations deftly
	• Builds productive relationships
	• May struggle with technical or detailed sales processes
	• May not always comply with rules and paperwork
Service Provider	• Exceptional troubleshooter
	• Empathizes with customers' situations
	• Listens actively but may become detached when unnecessary details or stories are involved
	• Understands ways to get things done outside conventional means
	• Very aware of protecting both parties interests
	• Resolves complaints quickly
	• Exudes confidence
Team Member	• Well liked by others
	• Prefers to be rewarded based on individual achievements
	• Gets results without creating ill will
	• Knows the rules; may not always follow them if they interfere with the goal
	• Works best when appreciated and given latitude to get things done
	• More likely to ask for forgiveness than permission
	• Aware of the morale of colleagues

THE SAGE

- Lowest score in column d
- Next lowest score in column a
- Warrior/Expert
- In a nutshell: "The system works; trust the system. The Sage has a system."

When I think of the Sage, I think of the Japanese term *kaizen* and the total quality management approach to business excellence that took root in the United States in the 1980s. These philosophies embraced the use of an established process to continuously evaluate and enhance the organization's systems to achieve greater efficiency and customer satisfaction. As the head of human resources and quality for a hotel management company, I was responsible for learning and applying these concepts. They require knowledge of several very technical approaches that organizations must adopt, apply, and continuously manage. It is a specific way of thinking. It is a *system*. And the Sage embraces a specific system for continuously enhancing performance, because he or she is:

- Thorough
- Process-driven
- Accurate
- Productive
- Quality-focused
- Values, controls, and metrics
- Direct
- Consistent
- Compliant
- Efficient
- Detailed
- Competitive

One of the telltale signs for me that the Sage is the most unsung of the styles is that it is the only one of the 12 icons that I don't share a story about during my seminars. I feel compelled to illustrate each style using a personal story, to connect my audience to one of my own life experiences reflecting an interaction with a person who communicates in that particular way. But the Sage doesn't stand out in this way—and that, I think, is the Sage's gift. Sages are life's pluggers. They methodically apply their system of thinking to each situation in an attempt to achieve greater reliability and obtain more results. They are not one to embrace the newest innovation without some very specific and factual evidence of its value.

Most of the Sages whom I have worked with—and remember distinctly—were my coaches. I wrote about one in some detail in my first book, *Live and Learn or Die Stupid!* This Sage was my high school baseball coach, Bob Gaddey. When he arrived at my high school during my senior year, we immediately butted heads. I now realize that my somewhat rebellious nature, unwillingness to subscribe to his approach, and touchy-feely tendencies placed me squarely in the role of nemesis to his steady, emotionless, play-by-the-book coaching style.

Since high school baseball season in southern Illinois was played in the spring and since spring weather in southern Illinois is about as predictable as a Lindsay Lohan weekend outing, we often had practice indoors in the basketball gym. Inevitably, we would end these practices with wind sprints, which are also known as suicides. Somehow, that name still doesn't capture the effect this conditioning drill has on your being. Suicides worked like this: You started at one end of the basketball court, ran to the near free throw line and back, ran to the half court line and back, ran to the far free throw line and back, and finally to the far end line and back. That was one suicide. One. We did *10. Then* we would keep running them until every member of the team finished the suicide at a specific time. I can't remember what that time was. Clearly, it is a repressed memory.

What I *do* remember is that I was not committed to my conditioning when I was a senior in high school. Let's just say that I violated several of the training rules on most nights. (Hey, there's not much to do in Greenup, Illinois, after baseball practice that doesn't involve violating a training rule.) Anyway, as a result of my lifestyle choices, I would run the first five or so suicides quite quickly—but with each of the last five, I got going slower and slower. After 10, I was done. Seriously, stick a fork in me. Of course, now it was time to run the timed suicides. Again, *everybody* had to finish the suicide at a specified time in order for *everybody* to finish practice. To be exceptionally clear, if even *one* person failed to finish the suicide in the prescribed time, everyone had to continue to run them.

Crap!

Inevitably, I would not finish in time. I still remember Coach Gaddey yelling, "Mitchell, you run like you have a piano on your back!" He knew (because he saw how quickly I *could* run a suicide) that my performance was not due to speed but due to conditioning. He knew I was breaking the training rules. He was engaged in a teaching moment; I was engaged in a heart attack.

It worked. Coach Gaddey knew that my need to be liked and not let down my teammates would drive me to pick up my conditioning. His system prevailed, as he knew it would. I tried to resist, but it was futile.

And that is the beauty of Sages. They can outwait you. They trust their knowledge. Sages may not be tactful or even likable sometimes, but they have the patience to allow their approach to yield fruit. *Kaizen*, baby!

As leaders, Sages exhibit the wisdom of their experience and confidence in the systems they've developed. Like the corner man for a boxer, they remind others to comply with the process and continuously look for ways to improve others' performance. They may not be warm and fuzzy, but they respect high performers who produce quality work.

As sales professionals, Sages approach their markets systematically. They work best within a clearly articulated strategy and structure that provides them with the foundation to work their territories. They have great depth of knowledge about their products and services and use this to assertively move the sales transaction toward closure.

As service providers, Sages are the consummate process-driven problem solvers. Their familiarity with the organization's offerings—combined with compliance to procedures—makes them low-risk, high-success troubleshooters. They may struggle with unique scenarios, but they will endeavor to learn the details to find a successful outcome.

Sages are steady, reliable, consistent, and determined team members. You can count on them to generate dependable results using existing organizational processes. They rarely make mistakes, and they excel in environments that value compliance and productivity.

The two Hollywood actors that come to mind for me when discussing the Sage are Gene Hackman and Dame Judi Dench. Gene, particularly in the movies *Hoosiers* and *The French Connection*, perfectly exhibited that plugger mentality. Sages may not be flashy, but they achieve success using a dogged persistence and belief in their own knowledge. In her role as M in the reboot of the James Bond movies, Judi displayed many of these same qualities. Despite criticism of her management style, she remained steadfast in her approach and her practices were later vindicated.

A more comic take on this style was provided by Robert De Niro in the movie *Meet the Parents*. His character, Jack Byrnes, describes his preference for cats over dogs to his future son-in-law with this line: "You see, Greg, when you yell at a dog, his tail will go between his legs and cover his genitals, his ears will go down. A dog is very easy to break, but cats make you work for their affection. They don't sell out the way dogs do." There's a person who has a very specific approach to pet selection. And, for the record, I prefer dogs.

Here's a quick reference guide for the Sage:

Role	Qualities
Leadership	• Committed to quality • Demands efficiency and continuous improvement • Rewards compliance and productivity • Provides no-nonsense feedback • Provides consistent and reliable management • Not particularly warm and fuzzy
Sales Professional	• Works the system • Organized in his or her approach to the market • Has great depth of knowledge of product and process • Productive plugger • Not generally a big relationship builder
Sales Provider	• Has thorough knowledge of products and services • Complies with organizational procedures • Very effective with common situations • May struggle when new products or services are introduced
Team Member	• Dependable producer • Follows rules • Works best in structured situations • Responds well to training • Once fully competent, can be trusted to produce accurate work • May resist change that does not appear to be well thought out

THE POWER BROKER

- Lowest score in column d
- Next lowest score in column c
- Warrior/Mastermind
- In a nutshell: "A force of nature who understands the vision and has a strategy for realizing it."

Power Brokers are the franchise players who *get things done.* They understand the vision and may have had a great deal of influence on its development. More important, they have a clear strategy for realizing this desired future state. They set aggressive goals and expect others to fulfill them. They have the power to push, pull, or drag the team to success. If necessary, they will load the team on their back and carry them to that goal, and when they get there (and they *will*), they will fire every miserable person who they had to carry. (Kidding. Sorta.)

The bottom line—and Power Brokers like the bottom line—is that this style wants to win and will relentlessly pursue victory. Power Brokers are the speedboats on the river of life. Heaven help you if you are in a canoe. There will be waves.

Here are a few words that would describe the Power Broker:

- Bold
- Strategic
- Productive
- Driven
- Results-oriented
- Impatient
- Forceful
- Direct
- Independent
- Powerful
- Fast
- Confident

One of the best ways to understand the Power Broker's mind-set is to imagine a metaphor involving the movement of a heavy cart from one location to the other. Let's imagine that there are two paths that the cart can travel. One path is clearly the most efficient but poses a risk of running over an unsuspecting bystander's foot. The other path will take longer to travel but poses no risk to others. Here is how four of the previously discussed styles might navigate this metaphor:

The Best Friend will know his way around both paths. Fearing any danger to others, he will sacrifice his own needs and take the less efficient path, thereby guaranteeing everyone's safety.

The Crusader will opt for the more efficient path. Once coming in contact with others, she will sacrifice her own needs by stopping and warning others of the potential danger.

The Hired Gun will opt for the more efficient path. Should he unintentionally run over someone's foot, he will apologize *after* the fact, thus ensuring maximum productivity while also maintaining a positive relationship.

The Power Broker will opt for the more efficient path. Should someone's foot be an unintended victim, she will ask, "What kind of idiot puts his foot in an aisle where heavy carts are traveling?"

Power Brokers are the engine of productivity. They are not interested in unnecessary details or learning the stories and minutiae involved in getting to a result. They care only about the *result*. "Tell me what you did, not what you plan to do," is a common refrain uttered by Power Brokers. Others include, "Nothing personal; its business," and "no news is good news." When they pass through an environment, they will leave casualties. The Best Friend often follows the Power Broker around, offering counseling to the injured. "He doesn't hate you; he hates everyone. You should hear how he talks to me, and he *likes* me," offers the Best Friend.

As leaders, Power Brokers are very comfortable working in the conceptual realm of a desired future state. Once Power Brokers and their teams have defined that vision, the Power

Broker is even more at home developing the strategies that will realize it. Power Brokers are direct, logical, demanding, and focused on aggressive goals. They reward others with independence and new challenges. They do not suffer fools gladly and will be assertive, maybe even aggressive, when eliminating poor performers.

As sales professionals, Power Brokers may be best working on the big deals. They enjoy seeing the big picture and developing a plan for achieving it. They are less interested in building personal relationships and care more about gaining access to people who can make big decisions. Although their direct style can occasionally hurt feelings, it does make them good at overcoming others' objections and closing quickly. They are not easily dissuaded from the goal they have set for themselves.

Power Brokers will be very direct service providers. They can identify a problem immediately and cut through any red tape to get a solution. They may not be particularly likable, but you can't deny their productivity. Their no-nonsense, to-the-point style will appeal to people who know what they want and expect to receive it without too much small talk and chitchat.

Power Brokers are natural team leaders in terms of ensuring that the team is making progress to their assigned goal. They can develop a reputation for not being team players; however, this generally comes as a result of Power Brokers not respecting team members for whom they don't have much use. They expect others to be good at what they do and will gravitate to those who have proved their value.

Hollywood loves the Power Broker. They chew the scenery. Think Jack Nicholson ("You can't *handle* the truth!" [Colonel Nathan R. Jessup from *A Few Good Men*]), Clint Eastwood ("Feel lucky, punk?" [*Dirty Harry*]), or Sigourney Weaver (*Alien, Aliens*). They are bold strokes of bright colors on a blank white canvas. Al Pacino may be the most iconic Power Broker of all time. In my opinion, the three greatest Al Pacino Power Broker movies are *The Godfather: Part II*, *Scarface*, and

The Devil's Advocate. Now, I am not comparing the Power Broker to an organized crime boss, a drug trafficker, or Satan. I'm just saying—these are powerful characters.

Here's a quick reference guide for the Power Broker:

Role	Qualities
Leadership	• Demands results • Gives independence to high performers; provides criticism and counseling for everyone else • Not big on praise • Has a clear vision and strategy • Writes rules; may not always follow them • Uninterested in details or unnecessary meetings • "Tell me what you did, not what you are going to do." • Believes success is measured by results • May be unaware of morale issues • Powerful • Provides direct, concise feedback
Sales Professional	• Problem solver • Can work around rules to get rapid results • Strong closer • Good at identifying and pursuing new clients • May not enjoy maintaining relationships with unproductive clients • May put pressure on operations to stretch capacity

(continued)

(*continued*)

Role	Qualities
Service Provider	• Must be careful not to rush to close rather than invest in relationship • Tells clients the solution • Resolves situations quickly • Willing to think outside the box to get the desired outcome • May not be sensitive to customers' emotional state
Team Member	• Very productive • May prefer to work alone rather than with a team

THE VOICE OF REASON

- Lowest score in column a
- Next lowest score in column b
- Expert/Romantic
- In a nutshell: "The steady Eddie who shows his or her compassion by teaching the correct way to avoid mistakes."

Voices of Reason are like math teachers. They are very good at explaining technical information or policies to others in a way that they understand. They care about others and provide them with the rules and details that will keep them from getting in trouble. They hold others accountable for compliance but do so with patience and tact. Although you may not realize how much they care, rest assured that compassion for others lies under their unwavering professionalism.

The Voice of Reason could be described as:

- Empathetic
- Cautious
- Detailed

- Diplomatic
- Reliable
- Technical
- Compliant
- Appropriate
- Consistent
- Professional
- Patient
- Conscientious

To best understand the nuances of the Voice of Reason, it is helpful to compare this style to a similar one: the Best Friend. The Voice of Reason is the Expert/Romantic, whereas the Best Friend is the Romantic/Expert. They have the same two interactive style preferences, simply reversed in order. Imagine each of these styles as a general practitioner. Now imagine that I have something wrong with me. Let's say . . . um . . . leprosy. I wake up in the morning and notice my ear has stuck to the pillow. I notice a hole in my cheek while I am shaving. My nose has slid substantially to the right side of my face. I say to myself, "Hmm, that's odd. I should have that checked." (It will probably be a few months because, after all, I am a man, and it takes a lot to get us to the doctor.)

Now, let's further imagine that I will visit both the Best Friend doctor and the Voice of Reason doctor. We'll start with the Best Friend doctor. I arrive for my appointment and am greeted by a very friendly staff that treat me like family. The atmosphere is very casual. I am ushered into the examining room right on time because the Best Friend doctor is quite punctual. As I enter the examining room, the Best Friend has her back to me. She is looking quite smashing in her crisp, white lab coat. As she turns around she says, "Hi, I am Doct—oh my God! Are you in pain? Oh, you poor thing. Please sit down."

Immediately, I am impressed by her compassion. It is clear that she cares deeply about me and my condition. However, I am also a little freaked out because of her emotional reaction. The emotional environment has been elevated in response to my situation. Such is the way of the Best Friend. They are adept counselors who are comfortable with this heightened emotional state.

Now let's imagine that I visit the Voice of Reason's practice. I also receive exceptional patient service at the office, but it is distinctly more formal. I am clearly a patient here, not a family member. I am again ushered into the examining room on time, because the Voice of Reason doctor is also a stickler about timeliness. As I enter the examining room, the Voice of Reason doctor also looks smashing in his white coat with a clipboard in hand. He turns toward me and says, "Hello, I am Dr. Voice of Reason. I will be your treating physician today. I have a 276-question diagnostic checklist that I use to determine the exact nature of your affliction."

It is right here that the Power Broker doctor would yell, "*Hello!* It's *leprosy.* I think we can nix the checklist there, Doctor VOR." Dr. Voice of Reason would respond, "That's exactly how a misdiagnosis can occur and why I complete the checklist for each patient."

"Do you have a fever?"

"No."

"Do you have a dry, hacking cough?"

"No."

"Do you have a runny nose? Hmm . . . I'm going to mark that yes."

After 30 minutes and 276 questions, the Voice of Reason doctor pronounces my affliction to be leprosy. The Power Broker doctor says, "Ya think? I have treated five patients in the time it took you to determine this patient has leprosy!"

"Yes," responds Dr. Voice of Reason, "but just last month a patient died due to your misdiagnosis."

"Meh, you lose a few. I go by volume," replies Dr. Power Broker.

The Voice of Reason relies on *compliance to proven methodology* to fulfill their desire to help others with their technical knowledge. They are reliable executors of precedence and steady and professional contributors to the team.

As leaders, Voices of Reason are technically proficient and committed to ensuring each team member knows and complies with the organization's policies, procedures, and processes. They often have depth of knowledge about the business's core functions and an excellent demeanor for delivering detailed training. They hold others accountable using a patient and tactful approach to employee coaching and counseling.

As sales professionals, Voices of Reason will follow a prescribed process for educating their customers about the benefits of their products and service and will develop respected relationships within their industry. They will retain a large portion of the customer base they capture but may need support in finding new business.

As service providers, Voices of Reason will have a comprehensive understanding of the products and services. They use this to both troubleshoot customer problems and better explain the features to facilitate greater client satisfaction. They will be compliant to company policies and will work within the prescribed level of authority to identify solutions to customer concerns.

As team members, Voices of Reason are well-respected, accurate, and knowledgeable contributors who strive to follow the rules and generate few mistakes. They care about the quality of their work, and their contentious nature may cause them to become defensive when criticized. They take their work seriously.

Although Voices of Reason may not be flashy characters in Hollywood, they are often portrayed as gracious, elegant, and appropriate. Tom Hanks played the epitome of this character in *Saving Private Ryan*. Cary Grant and Matt Damon have also captured the essence of the Voice of Reason on screen. For women, Gwyneth Paltrow, Audrey Hepburn, and Jodie Foster all have embodied the intellect, grace, and refinement that are hallmarks of this style.

Here's a quick reference guide for the Voice of Reason:

Role	Qualities
Leadership	• Structured • Technical educator • Compliant to policies, processes, and systems • Appreciative of others • Values accuracy and quality • Uncomfortable with chaos • Risk averse • Thorough communicator
Sales Professional	• Builds relationships based on respect • Has deep knowledge of products and services • Steady • Maintains existing client base • Provides accurate expectations to clients
Service Provider	• Provides accurate information • Understands how products and services work • Teaches others how to use products and services • Cares about client satisfaction • Stays within assigned level of authority
Team Member	• Reliable performer • Respected colleague • Rarely makes mistakes • Uncomfortable with criticism • Prefers highly structured and appreciative environments • Good team player

THE SPECIALIST

- Lowest score in column a
- Next lowest score in column d
- Expert/Warrior
- In a nutshell: "Perfection. No surprises. They like right and on time."

They are, in a word, *perfect*. That's in their delusion, of course. Specialists take great pride in both the quality of their work and their ability to deliver it on time. If you liked their work yesterday, you will like it today and you will like it tomorrow. If you didn't like their work yesterday, you won't like it today and you won't like it tomorrow. Maybe *you* need to change your expectations. One of the most reliable performers, they are rigidly compliant to what they believe to be the best practices for their craft.

Here are a few words that would describe the Specialist:

- Compliant
- Knowledgeable
- Strict
- Detailed
- Perfectionist
- Process-oriented
- Quality-focused
- Direct
- Reliable
- Stubborn
- Correct
- Trustworthy

My most significant memory involving a group of Specialists takes place in Texas in the late 1990s and involves 35 chemical engineers. I had been hired by the training department to conduct a seminar on communication. (Who would have imagined that a group of chemical engineers would need training on communication?) Anyway, I arrived at the plant 45 minutes before the seminar as I usually do and was escorted to the training room by the receptionist.

I have never seen an actual prison cell, but I would imagine that most would be more creatively decorated than this training room. In fact, a prison cell would be practically Ralph Lauren–esque by comparison. The style could best be described as "early '70s functional." The walls were stark white, and the only wall hanging was the whiteboard in the front of the room. The chairs were arranged classroom style, with one solitary 6-foot table placed front and center. I unpacked my laptop and hooked it up to the LCD projector, which back then was roughly the size of a pinball machine. By 8:30 AM I had completed my preseminar preparation and readied myself for greeting the attendees for the 9:00 AM start.

8:45 AM—no attendees.
8:50 AM—no attendees.
8:55 AM—no attendees.

Now I was beginning to panic. Did I have the right time? Did I have the right date? Was I in the right room? This was before the advent of smartphones, so I was unable to verify any information quickly. My heart raced. But just as I was ready to dash down the hall to the receptionist, here they came: 35 chemical engineers entering the training room single file at precisely 8:58 AM. With the focus and surety inherent in the Specialist style, they walked silently to their respective chairs, sat down, opened their notebooks, and prepared to be educated.

Although I don't think they were wearing a company-issued uniform, the consistency of fashion choices was striking. Khaki pants paired with a short-sleeved dress shirt with a T-shirt underneath. Many wore glasses that from a distance had a geek chic, vintage coolness. However, I realized as I got closer that the glasses were just old, some being held together by transparent tape. The whole scene could have been taken straight from a 1960s NASA documentary. I swallowed hard and thought to myself, "This should be really interesting."

I began the session. Anyone reading this book who has seen me speak knows that I put a lot of humor and energy into my seminars. But each time I hit a punch line that had resulted in raucous laughter at previous events, I got nothing—not so much as a giggle and certainly no guffaws. I was 1 hour into the 3-hour seminar and the audience was colder than a Siberian cellar.

When things are not going well I usually respond by throwing more energy into it. I can hear the voice in my head saying, "Oh *hell* no! You are going to have fun!" I amped up my delivery. I was Richard Simmons on methamphetamines. I was running up and down, side to side inside the room. The attendees were leaning back in their chairs offering a nonverbal communication that equated to, "Dude, take a Prozac and a nap." After 3 hours, exhausted, I ended the session still having received nary a smile, let alone a chuckle. I went to the door to thank them for coming and resigned myself to having taken one on the chin.

They lined up like it was a wedding reception and I was the new bride. One by one each of the 35 chemical engineers (Specialists) walked up to me and said some variation of, "That was the best seminar that I have ever attended." All I could think was, "Tell your face."

Of course, the real lesson was meant for me. As an educator, my job is to achieve the transfer of learning, successfully introducing concepts that my "student" can absorb, connect with, and apply. It is not my audience's responsibility to fulfill my intrinsic need, quite the opposite, in fact. What I *had* done effectively was provide these Experts with a model for understanding one of the most conceptual issues that we humans experience: communication with one another. The fact that they didn't fall out of their chairs laughing or jump to their feet in spontaneous applause was a *me* issue, not a *them* issue. Sometimes the teacher becomes the student right in the middle of the lesson.

The Specialists are a serious lot. They have high standards for how things should be done and expect it to happen on or ahead of deadline. They use their experiences to guide the approach they have to their craft. They trust what they have seen, heard, smelled, tasted, or touched. Anything else is hooey. It is that quality that makes them so good at what they do and also very rigid.

As leaders, Specialists are all about quality and structure. They set up systems meant to eliminate mistakes and expect others to comply with them without exception. They use their great depth of knowledge to mentor others on their craft, and they command respect because of their consistency and reliability.

Specialist sales professionals work the system using detailed product knowledge and exceptional ability to identify problems and offer credible solutions. They keep their promises, accurately depict their capabilities, and build relationships based on trust.

Specialists are cautious but results-oriented service providers who thoroughly explain the process and do exactly what they tell you they will do. They take pride in both doing things correctly and being efficient.

As team members, Specialists are no-nonsense contributors who thrive in tightly defined roles. They are compliant to the rules and committed to knowing everything about their jobs. They can be trusted to deliver a high quality of work in an expedited manner.

Hollywood generally casts the Specialist as a role player. Think of the safe cracker or the computer hacker in a crime caper or the munitions expert in a war movie. There have been leading roles, too. Jeremy Renner's version of Bourne and Jodie Foster in *Silence of the Lambs* are great examples of Specialists. Harvey

Keitel as Winston "The Wolf" Wolfe in *Pulp Fiction* is iconic in the role as the Specialist. Gillian Anderson also portrayed one in *The X-Files* with her no-nonsense, well-reasoned character Dana Scully.

Here's a quick reference guide for the Specialist:

Role	Qualities
Leadership	• Very structured • Expects compliance to policies and systems • Demands quality • Is efficient and productive • Mentors others with knowledge • Holds people accountable • Rewards others with security and space
Sales Professional	• Understands the capabilities of products and services • Keeps promises • Carefully evaluates customers' needs • Works a proven sales process • Completes paperwork accurately and on time
Service Provider	• Understands the capabilities of products and services • Keeps promises • Carefully evaluates customers' needs • Works a proven sales process • Completes paperwork accurately and on time
Team Member	• Steady, consistent, and reliable performer • Rarely makes mistakes • Thrives in well-defined situations • Comfortable with repetitive tasks

THE DETECTIVE

- Lowest score in column a
- Next lowest score in column c
- Expert/Mastermind
- In a nutshell: "Brilliant or loopy? Yes. The Detective can be either and both, but don't dismiss a Detective's ideas no matter how offbeat."

The Detective will cure cancer some day. Unfortunately, no one will understand what the Detective is talking about. This style combines the Expert's focus and detailed approach with the Mastermind's risk tolerance and conceptual mind. That frees the Detective to experiment with processes and work outside of systems, but in a methodical and replicable way. Detectives are like the mad scientists in the laboratory, combining existing concoctions in creative ways to see what happens. It could be amazing—or it might explode.

Here are a few words that would describe the Detective:

- Knowledgeable
- Quirky
- Creative
- Conceptual
- Research-based
- Unconventional
- Thorough
- Enthusiastic
- Unpredictable
- Experimental
- Different
- Specific

When I developed the program *The Power of Understanding People—Hollywood Style*, I initially noticed a disturbing phenomenon. During the first nearly five years of delivering the seminar, not one single person has a result in this style. *Not one.* Approximately 50,000 participants from a diverse array of organizations had attended my seminars—and not a single Detective had emerged. I became concerned that there was a hole in the assessment. However, those concerns were replaced by bemusement during a visit to a software company in Houston, Texas. It was there that I ran into a herd, a covey, a pride, a flock—whatever a group of Detectives calls themselves.

I had been hired to provide presentation skills training to a group of research and development (R&D) professionals at this company. I do several presentation skills classes each year, so there is nothing unusual about that situation. Sure, this particular group of seven R&D guys (and they were all guys) happened to be exceptionally smart and very wealthy. Each had negotiated an employment contract that allowed him to maintain some ownership over his software. But it was not the situation nor intellect and net worth of the participants that made this exceptional: It was their *style*. All seven of these men were Detectives.

I suspected something was different the moment they arrived at the session. You see, presentation skills training is an unusually stressful seminar for most people. After all, public speaking routinely outranks death when people are asked about things they most fear. This class not only requires the attendees to speak publicly but entails them doing so in front of a professional who is critiquing them in the presence of their peers. Oh, and did I mention that we video record the entire thing? It's hell on earth for almost everyone. So the one thing you can count on is that the attendees have spent quality time making their wardrobe decisions. Hey, if you are going to be on display facing your greatest fear and have a video document of the occasion, you at least want to look sharp.

As the seven students arrived for the two-day course, I noticed a certain commonality in their appearance. I wouldn't go so far as calling their attire a *uniform,* but the number of common components was rather compelling. First, there was the hairstyle. It is a style we lovingly refer to here in the mountains of Colorado where I live as the skullet. The skullet is a modified mullet: no hair on top and a ponytail in the back. And although it rocks on a Harley-Davidson, it is somewhat uncommon in a corporate setting. Rock band T-shirts were a popular choice, too; Grateful Dead for those older than 50; Phish or Widespread Panic for those younger.

And then there were the pants, which weren't actually pants; they were shorts. Jean shorts. *Self-cut* jean shorts. Self-cut one leg at a time, resulting in both the uneven hemline and, alarmingly in one case, a far too aggressive cut. I knew when he was walking down the hallway toward the classroom and I could see the majority of his front pocket *underneath* the hemline that if he sat at the front of the class, I was going to learn far too much about him.

When you are rocking the sweet skullet, tie-dye Grateful Dead T-shirt, and self-cut jean shorts, you put an inordinate amount of pressure on your footwear selection. It becomes the focal point of your ensemble. Five of the seven participants opted for the highly controversial Birkenstock/sock combination. Now, I do not endorse this fashion choice, but I have to admit as a Coloradan that I have become somewhat desensitized to it. So it wasn't that alone that had me riveted to the train wreck that was the first presenter's feet. Nope. It was the color—or should I say, *colors*—of his socks. He had one periwinkle blue sock and one forest green sock. Periwinkle blue and forest green are two completely different colors. Even in the absence of light, one can discern between periwinkle blue and forest green. Helen Keller could have gotten closer!

Remember, I am a Crusader: the somewhat conflicted style formed by a combination of Romantic and Warrior. By the way, that makes the Detective the style that I most struggle to understand. My Romantic schema was telling me to overlook this individual's unusual fashion choices and just smile and encourage him. Unfortunately, my Warrior schema could allow me to do no such thing. The Warrior's direct and results-oriented approach would override my tact and diplomacy on this occasion. Right in the middle of his presentation, I blurted out, "Do you realize that your socks are two completely different colors?"

And that is when it happened. My world was about to be truly transformed. At that precise moment, I felt like I traveled through a wormhole to an alternative universe. I became aware that all seven of these individuals were Detectives. It was clear when each of them turned toward me with a look of befuddlement regarding my question. There was a moment of hesitation as the speaker considered what appeared to be a puzzling question to him. And then came his response.

"I go by thickness."

(Silence.)

I was 39 years old when this happened. My first job in media was as a disc jockey at the college radio station when I was 18 years old. Ever since that time, I had always been in professions that required me to be verbally nimble, quick on my feet, and ready with a witty retort. I had nothing. "I go by thickness" had hit my brain at such an oblique angle that I couldn't process it. As a result, I "blue screened"—my brain hard-booting like a viral-ridden laptop computer. My default settings were restored and apparently my primal response in these conditions is to simply repeat what I last heard.

"You go by thickness," I said.

"Yes, I go by thickness." The Detective speaker had the faintest hint of condescension in his tone, perhaps even a little disdain. What he didn't have was even a shred of sarcasm or humor. He was serious.

"You go by thickness," I repeated, still trying to install my customized cognitive settings. Still no witty retort file located.

Resigned to having to explain what he felt was infinitely obvious, the Detective continued. "The primary purpose of the sock is to provide a barrier between your foot and your shoe. Critical to its functionality is the thickness of the sock. The sock's value depends on the comfort provided by the thickness. The color of a sock is merely an aesthetic element, has virtually no real value, and is not something I consider when making a sock selection."

(Silence again.)

You can't argue with that reasoning. That is *solid*. At that moment, my cognitive settings were fully restored and I realized that my sock selection process was based on how *I* look and what others think of me—a distinctly Romantic and Warrior perspective. The Detective's sock selection was based on practicality and was not encumbered by others' expectations. In fact, of the two approaches, the Detective's selection process makes far more sense. He can buy tube socks of a variety of colors and need only worry that one sock may be without a partner at any given time. My selection process has left me with about eight single socks lying on top of my dresser awaiting their partner's return. How does that happen? Was there some form of footwear domestic dispute in the washing machine that resulted in one sock moving out? Seriously, where do these socks *go*? It's an issue that most of us face—but one that this Detective never deals with.

I am not suggesting that all Detectives wear mismatched socks. (However, when I told this story at a Sub-Zero Wolf training session in Madison, Wisconsin, some years back, the Detective in the audience actually did have two different colors of socks on. Given that they were navy blue and black, I think that was more the result of low lighting in the laundry room than an unconventional sock selection process.) What I am suggesting is that the Detectives will cure cancer someday, because they have an incredible ability to apply existing processes in creative ways.

As leaders, Detectives inspire others with their depth of knowledge and willingness to take calculated chances. They push technical people in creative directions by providing a framework of structure that can be applied in new ways. They have a methodology for exploration.

As sales professionals, Detectives use an established sales process to identify new opportunities. They find unconventional markets for their products and services. They are detailed and thorough, yet comfortable exploring new situations and applications for what they sell.

Detective service providers can always find a way to apply policies and procedures to even the most uncommon customer problem. They are comfortable defending their solutions, not as precedent, but as a natural extension of an existing approach. They are creative but compliant.

Detectives may not be the most conventional communicators as team members; they may appear to introduce unusual topics unrelated to the current discussion. However, if you pay attention, these ideas often have incredible merit if you allow yourself to think outside the box. More accurately, allow Detectives to introduce a *new* box—this is where they excel.

The Detective is generally portrayed by a somewhat quirky character in films. Sherlock Holmes was always able to arrive at creative solutions by paying close attention to the details. The title characters in *Monk, Columbo*, and *House M.D.* are Detectives who have been featured on television programs. MacGyver made the combination of technical knowledge and creativity into a weekly plot device. Each character possesses a great depth of expertise and displays these skills in unusual ways. In the television show *Bones*, Emily Deschanel's Dr. Temperance Brennan combines science and geekiness to create forensic genius. Robert Downey Jr.'s *Iron Man* is another example of what happens when the Expert and Mastermind style combine.

Here's a quick reference guide for the Detective:

Role	Qualities
Leadership	• Technically proficient • Offers structured creativity • Risk aware and uses policies and procedures to mitigate the possibility of mistakes • Leads by example • Unconventional • Comfortable applying policies and processes in new ways
Sales Professional	• Uses a process • Comfortable in both existing and new markets • Sells with knowledge and flexibility • Acts as consultant on technical matters
Service Provider	• Solves problems by combining a deep knowledge of products and services with a willingness to be creative • Enjoys a complicated issue • Not overly personable, gains respect by understanding issues and persistently pursuing a fix
Team Member	• Provides both ideas and structure • May be a little socially clunky • Excellent support for both Romantics and Warriors • Comfortable working independently • Knows policies, procedures, and processes but may apply them in unusual ways • May come across as a little geeky about his or her area of expertise

THE ECCENTRIC

- Lowest score in column c
- Next lowest score in column a
- Mastermind/Expert
- In a nutshell: "The savvy crisis manager, the Eccentric can make the unreal become real. Marketing genius and 'nuttier than an elephant burp.'"

When I read the quote above in a newspaper in Phoenix, used to describe mountain bikers, I immediately thought of the Eccentric. Eccentrics are one of the most intriguing styles for me. When I listen to them talk about the future, they present a very compelling argument that the unreal can become real. They are masters of recreating the perception of a situation into something completely different than you think. My favorite Hollywood Eccentric is Johnny Depp's Captain Jack Sparrow from *Pirates of the Caribbean*. Somehow he manages to convince others of his gravitas as a pirate captain despite the obvious limitations of having no crew, no ship, and no treasure. He doesn't even have a parrot. But what he *does* have is a vision . . . and the correct wardrobe.

Here are a few words that would describe the Eccentric:

- Energetic
- Passionate
- Process-oriented
- Uncommon
- Risk tolerant
- Entrepreneurial
- Detailed
- Conceptual
- Eccentric (I know, that's cheating)
- Inspiring

- Unconventional
- Unique

In the previous section about the Detective, I admitted that because that style uses the two interactive tools that are my least preferred, I struggle most to connect with them. The Eccentric also uses my two least preferred tools, in the opposite order: Mastermind and Expert. For this reason, the style can also be challenging for me to understand. In fact, having worked with an example of this style when I was a human resources executive, I can share a specific story of how I learned the genius of the Eccentric.

The vice president of sales and marketing (who I shall refer to as VPSM) at the Buena Vista Hospitality Group was said person, and I was the vice president of human resources and quality. Every day the two of us and the rest of the executive committee would meet at 5:00 PM to discuss issues affecting the hotels and ensure that we were aligned as a leadership team. When you meet every single day, at the end of your workday, these meetings can become tedious. There is a lot of pressure to say something meaningful and say it succinctly. There are also some very overt behavioral cues that everyone wants to go home. Inevitably, just as it appeared the meeting was winding down and all of us were organizing our papers and preparing to leave the boardroom, VPSM would introduce some unusual topic. He wouldn't bring up a simple yes/no scenario but rather a topic that would have kept Socrates busy for a week.

Our president: Well, unless any one has anything else to dis—
VPSM: Bob, have we thought about intelligent guest room software?
Our president: I don't know what that is, VPSM.
VPSM: Well, I happened to read an article in *Scientific American* last week about cutting-edge technology that allows guests to check in using only their credit cards. This card then serves as

their room key during their stay. The guest can actually program the room's temperature controls, televisions channels . . . *(blah, blah, blah)*

Another hour would pass as we discussed that issue. Now, keep in mind that this conversation was occurring at 6:00 PM— *10 hours* into our workday. Keep in mind, too, that few of us in that room actually gave a crap about intelligent guest room software. Oh, and also keep in mind that the *Internet had not even been introduced to the public*—meaning that this idea was at least a decade away from even being *feasible*.

I hated him.

Okay, maybe not *hate*. He was a pretty good guy, actually, but his timing always irritated me. Add to that, most of what he said made little sense to me. Others didn't seem to mind so much, but for me it was complete lunacy. In fairness to VPSM, our sales had never been better, which was a fact I simply chalked up to good fortune. I figured he was a mediocre leader propped up by a talented staff. The people who worked for VPSM seemed to like him, another fact that I found hard to reconcile. They often spoke of his amazing intellect. I just found him to be a goofball— that is, until the fateful FAM trip at the Buena Vista Palace Resort and Spa.

A FAM trip (short for familiarization trip) is a common part of the sales process for a convention hotel. Often, when a meeting planner is considering bringing an event to a hotel, the property will arrange to bring that meeting professional in to visit at no charge. The goal, of course, is to for the hotel to impress the meeting planner and win his or her business. This particular FAM trip involved three meeting planners for a Fortune 100 company who were looking for one site to host a series of President's Councils. The amount of revenue was in the millions of dollars. It was a huge piece of business, and our hotel was one of only two properties being considered. Unfortunately, the other one was a brand new, not yet opened hotel: the Venetian in Las Vegas, which would become the largest five-diamond hotel in history.

The Venetian is amazing. It's not just a convention hotel; it is a *city*. It has an *entire mall* inside it. Guests can experience a Venice-like float through water canals inside it. There is a huge casino, a seemingly infinite number of restaurants and bars, a spa, and a huge pool area inside it. Major talents appear in their performance auditorium. Mario Batali and Wolfgang Puck hang out there to cook for people. The Venetian is larger than life, even by Las Vegas standards. Our hotel looked like a Motel 6 by comparison. We knew we couldn't compete fairly with this future titan of hospitality, so we decided to do what any self-respecting hotelier does when it can't compete fairly: We opened wine—and lots of it.

The entire executive team was recruited to host the FAM trip with the client. Nine vice president–level executives would accompany the three meeting planners for a tour of our property, which we decided to do at the end of the visit. First, we would ply the guest with first-growth Bordeaux wine and copious amounts of beef. Our strategy was to get the meeting planners liquored up and get a signed contract before they even made it to Las Vegas. That plan may have worked, too, had one of the meeting planners not stayed sober. Alas, he did not drink and insisted on touring the property before signing a contract. *So close.*

The next day, nine hung-over hoteliers, and two hung-over (and one perky . . . damn him!) meeting planners began the tour of our property led by VPSM. I remember thinking that VPSM was more charming than I expected. The tour was actually going nicely—that is, until we arrived at the escalators. Those damn escalators.

That day, of all days, was the day that the up escalator—the one that carried convention guests up *three stories* to our lobby area—was not working. Today, the conventioneers were walking up the escalator. This, on the day we are trying to impress three influential meeting planners. Seriously, have you ever seen people walk up a broken escalator? *Three flights?* It's like a death march.

Each of us executives turned the corner, saw the broken escalator, and immediately averted our eyes in horror. We all knew the ramifications of this development. No responsible meeting planner is going to recommend a hotel for a huge event when said hotel may have an intermittent escalator problem. Even though this may be a completely exceptional issue, a meeting planner simply wouldn't take the chance, particularly when these meeting planners had an alternative like the Venetian. We were screwed. Every one of us knew that.

Every one of us, that is, except the Eccentric VPSM.

VPSM walked to the base of the broken escalator and began discussing the flexibility of our largest ballroom. He seemed completely oblivious to the issue behind him. He enthusiastically presented the various configurations and room setups that the ballroom could accommodate. Finally, one of the meeting planners interrupted.

"I'm sorry. You have been very generous hosts. The wine and meal last night was over the top. However, I can't recommend a hotel that even has the possibility of an escalator problem." We all nodded quietly, except the VPSM, the Eccentric. What followed was about the most amazing example of persuasiveness I have experienced in 52 years of life. I can't explain it. I can only tell you that it was compelling.

"Ah, I see you have noticed our decorative steel staircase," VPSM began. "Not only is this an aesthetic marvel, it is also quite an engineering feat. With the mere touch of a button this entire staircase converts into a fully functional escalator. Now, of course, there is a daily service charge of $500 for that option, but depending on your food and beverage choices at the large events, I can probably work with you on that." He said this without the faintest hint of humor, sarcasm, or even insanity. I was there. I believed him.

Approximately two beats of silence passed before one of the meeting planners turned to the other two and said, "Given the size of our groups, I think we will need the escalator option." Oh. My. GOD. It worked! Now, I left to start my own company shortly after this experience, so I don't know if we actually won the contract. But the fact that it was still possible was nothing short of a miracle.

After the FAM trip, I went to VPSM's office. "That was amazing," I said.

"What?"

"What! You know, the whole 'decorative steel staircase that converts to a fully functional escalator with a mere touch of a button.'"

"I'm not following you."

And that's when it hit me. The reason VPSM's response had been so persuasive was that *he believed it*. In his delusion, that *was* a decorative steel staircase with the capacity to become an escalator. He could make the unreal become real. And *that* is why he was such a talented sales and marketing professional. His ability to combine conceptual ideas with practical explanation made possibilities compelling. It also ran perpendicular to my delusion of emotion and logic. The Eccentric is a great crisis manager and great marketing mind. Have you ever watched a Super Bowl commercial and asked yourself, who would spend millions of dollars on *that*? My bet is that the Eccentric sold it to whoever agreed to buy it.

As leaders, Eccentrics are both visionaries and pragmatists. They seek a desired future state that they can arrive at using all of the existing structure. They inspire by providing optimism and reassuring others that all the resources necessary for success already surround them.

As sales professionals, Eccentrics' depth of knowledge and unwavering faith in a positive outcome make them very persuasive. They are not dissuaded by objections and remain persistent in the face of rejection. Their unshakable belief in the ability of their products and/or services is infectious.

As service providers, Eccentrics are creative problem solvers who can find new and different ways to use the system to achieve the desired result. They mitigate risk with structure and use policies and procedures to achieve innovative outcomes.

As team members, Eccentrics are charismatic, if sometimes unconventional, contributors who will be comfortable in loosely defined situations while quickly establishing their own processes for ensuring quality. Although their ideas may appear radical, they can support them with compelling data.

Hollywood loves a good Eccentric. Virtually every superhero movie has a couple of them. He or she might be the evil genius or perhaps a hero. The aforementioned Johnny Depp is a great example. Val Kilmer as Doc Holliday in *Tombstone* was the Eccentric, as is virtually anything John Malkovich has ever played. In fact, both he and Glenn Close play Eccentrics in *Dangerous Liaisons*. (And leave it to an Eccentric woman to be named Glenn.) The Sheldon Cooper character on *Big Bang Theory* also comes to mind. Tina Fey pulls off a comedic version on *30 Rock*, as does Jennifer Coolidge as Stifler's mom in *American Pie*. Like I said, Hollywood loves the Eccentric.

Here's a quick reference guide for the Eccentric:

Role	Qualities
Leadership	• An excellent agent for change • Structured but flexible • Innovative but cautious • Able to provide data to support new directions • Unconventional
Sales Professional	• Enthusiastic about product and service capabilities

(continued)

(continued)

Role	Qualities
	• Persuasive and persistent
	• Has deep product knowledge
	• Comfortable using structure to pursue new markets
Service Provider	• Fearless problem solver
	• Knowledgeable about policies and procedures
	• Will get creative in providing technical support
Team Member	• Comfortable in loosely defined situations
	• Reliable, if unconventional, performer
	• May specialize in unusual responsibilities
	• May work best on his or her own rather than in a team

THE SOCIAL REFORMER

- Lowest score in column c
- Next lowest score in column b
- Mastermind/Romantic
- In a nutshell: "I have a dream! And it will benefit the people."

The Social Reformer is like a beloved king or queen. Social Reformers have a vision for the future that will enhance the lives of their people. It will make them healthier, wealthier, and happier. All you need to do is *believe*. They simply ask for a passionate commitment to their ideas. Their conceptual mind and emotional sensitivity make them charismatic leaders who others want to follow. They are tactful and diplomatic and share a future that is optimistic and appealing. What's not to like?

Well, there can be a little issue with details and strategies.

Here are a few words that describe the Social Reformer:

- Passionate
- Caring
- Visionary
- Diplomatic
- Charming
- Conceptual
- Empathetic
- Risk tolerant
- Enthusiastic
- Fun-loving
- Inspirational
- Dreamer

Social Reformers love to address their people. They emerge from their chambers onto their balcony, where the assembled masses wait with great anticipation to hear the latest description of an exciting and positive future toward which they are headed. They all listen in rapt attention as the Social Reformer shares the vision. They all are committed to supporting its realization.

There is one malcontent, however. That malcontent is the Specialist.

The Specialist listens closely for the details and strategies that will ensure that we achieve this desired future state—and she doesn't hear anything. The version of the future seems to be constructed from haze and hope. There is no *plan*. And without any tangible evidence of a process within which we can move from today to tomorrow as envisioned by the Social Reformer, the Specialist is unconvinced and therefore uncommitted.

"Pack of lies, pack of lies," exclaims the Specialist, right in the middle of the presentation. "Ask the Social Reformer about the details of his vision. They got nothing. Ask about the strategy for implementation. Zip. Pack of lies, pack of lies!"

The Social Reformer ignores the Specialist's screams and continues to share his vision. However, upon completion of the presentation, the Social Reformer turns to his trusted assistant—maybe the Crusader or the Hired Gun—and says, "Could you go find the Specialist for me? I would like a private audience."

The Crusader knows this doesn't bode well for the Specialist, but believing the Social Reformer's vision, exits to fetch the Specialist, with a growing sense of dread for what is to come. If the trusted aide to the Social Reformer is the Hired Gun, then there is the small matter of the contract. The Hired Gun reminds the Social Reformer that there is a $100 fee to fetch someone. As soon as the fee is paid, the fetching begins.

The Specialist goes willingly to the meet the Social Reformer, believing that—finally—she will have a chance to share with His Highness her concerns about the lack of tactics and plans. Upon arriving, the Specialist is disappointed to discover that the purpose of the meeting is for the Social Reformer to review the vision and once again ask the Specialist for her commitment. The Specialist will not commit without structure; the Social Reformer is not interested in structure unless the Specialist commits. There is a stalemate.

The Specialist is patient but not tactful. She will argue the contrary position for as long as necessary. The Social Reformer is tactful but not patient. He grows weary and bored with this conversation. Finally, the Social Reformer rises and says, "Well, Specialist, it appears we will have to agree to disagree. Thank you for coming up to meet with me. Have a nice day. Buh-bye." As the Social Reformer leaves the room, he walks by his trusted assistant.

"Have her beheaded."

The Social Reformer doesn't carry weaponry. Social Reformers don't kill; they have people who do it for them. The Crusader will accompany the Specialist to the gallows, the whole time saying, "Are you happy? Who speaks out in the middle of a meeting? We all have concerns about the plan, but we don't yell 'Pack of lies, pack of lies' in the middle of a meeting." *Whack*.

Afterward, the Crusader takes three days off to recover from the duress of the execution.

The Hired Gun reminds the Social Reformer that although it's $100 to fetch the Specialist, it's another $100 to execute them. On the way to the gallows, the Hired Gun turns to the Specialist and says, "So, do you know any other people who feel like you do?" (The Hired Gun works off referrals.)

The charismatic Social Reformer envisions a beautiful future for the people that can be accomplished only if we all truly and passionately believe in that dream. The Social Reformer fears that the malcontent will undermine the vision.

As leaders, Social Reformers are change agents. They imagine a better future for their employees and customers. They are comfortable taking chances and are eager to learn, even from mistakes. They are charismatic and well liked and are rarely annoyed by others—unless, of course, it's a malcontent or a nonbeliever.

As sales professionals, Social Reformers are both enthusiastic promoters of their products and services and adept relationship builders. They thrive in loosely defined situations, so they often seek new markets or customer bases. They find creative, appealing ways to position their goods and maintain optimism even when meeting with initial barriers.

Social Reformers are empathetic service providers. They use their energy and positive outlook to exude a can-do demeanor. This enthusiasm is often contagious and creates delighted customers. They may not always comply with policies, but this is generally because they're unaware they even existed.

As team members, Social Reformers are charismatic colleagues who care about the morale that surrounds them. They are comfortable offering ideas for enhancing the workplace and improving the team's situation. They loved to be inspired and to be helpful to others.

Social Reformers believe in people and are passionate, charismatic leaders who are fully committed to their dreams. Cate Blanchett (Queen Elizabeth), Meryl Streep (Karen Silkwood), and Julia Roberts (Erin Brockovich) have all played the role. Male Social Reformers include Denzel Washington (Malcolm X), Robert Redford (Henry Brubaker), and Peter O'Toole (Lawrence of Arabia). Each of these performance marked by a main character committed to social change.

Here's a quick reference guide for the Social Reformer:

Role	Qualities
Leadership	• Has a high risk tolerance • A visionary for social issues • Compassionate, particularly for believers • Appreciates others • More focused on desired future state than on structure • An agent for change, especially to benefit people
Sales Professional	• Sells with enthusiasm • Paints a picture of the impact of his or her product and services on people • Builds relationships • Comfortable finding new markets • Passionate about what he or she represents
Service Provider	• Comfortable working with a wide variety of customers • Empathetic to others • Creative problem solver • May take unconventional path to achieve result

Role	Qualities
Team Member	• Enthusiastic • Team player • Contributes ideas • Works to enhance morale • Comfortable in loosely defined situations • Loves new projects

THE ADVENTURER

- Lowest score in column c
- Next lowest score in column d
- Mastermind/Warrior
- In a nutshell: "Boldly go where no man has gone before."

If a style could be a poster child for an entrepreneur, it would be the Adventurer. Whereas the Power Broker gets things done within the framework of the organization, the Adventurer prefers to operate on the outside. Adventurers are all about discovery, but not just *any* discovery: It has be a discovery that *has value* and *can be implemented*. They are both conceptual and logical, so they are not prone to flights of fancy. They don't get excited about an idea until they can imagine a clear strategy for realizing it. It's this quality that often allows them to succeed.

Here are a few words that would describe the Adventurer:

- Daring
- Strategic
- Driven
- Entrepreneurial
- Creative
- Conceptual
- Direct
- Results-oriented
- Exciting

- Comfortable in chaos
- Independent
- Inspirational

I love *Star Trek*, especially the classic, corny 1960s *Star Trek*. In fact, I believe that some of the unexpected and sustained appeal of this franchise has to do with some crafty casting. I mean, when you watch the original television series, it's hard to imagine the audience fell in love with the cheesy special effects, wooden acting, and fairly uninspired plot lines. I think the appeal of the series has a lot to do with the four main characters: Bones McCoy, Mr. Spock, Scotty, and Captain James T. Kirk. Those four characters reflect the four interactive styles: Romantic, Warrior, Expert, and Mastermind, respectively.

Think about it. Do you remember any episode of *Star Trek* that didn't involve an overemoting Bones McCoy busting onto the command deck under tremendous duress or him exclaiming to Captain Kirk, "Damn it, Jim, I'm a doctor not a coal miner!" And who was most irritated by the pure emotionless logic of Mr. Spock? That's right: the Romantic McCoy. I also imagine that the Expert Scotty got pretty tired of having to repair or enhance the *Enterprise*. The man was a technical genius. I think even he knew there were dilithium crystals on undiscovered planets. Now that is an Expert.

And finally, there was Captain James T. Kirk. He was not only a Mastermind but an Adventurer. I created an entire backstory for Captain Kirk. I actually think J.J. Abrams, the director of the rebooted *Star Trek* franchise, may have attended one of my seminars, given how his backstory was somewhat similar to mine. *(Delusions of grandeur.)*

In my version, James Kirk was a rebellious but talented cadet at the Starfleet Academy. Although he exhibited tremendous potential and was admired by his fellow cadets, he was unpredictable and considered a dangerous rogue by the Federation Council. This created a dilemma. If the council were to graduate Kirk, they risked having a loose cannon released into the cosmos. However, if they did not graduate this talented and admired cadet, it would be demotivating to the other cadets. I imagine quite a deliberation between the president and vice president of the Federation Council, with the president as the Voice of Reason and the vice president as the Sage.

"I am very conflicted over the future of Cadet Kirk," says the Voice of Reason. "To graduate him will put many at great risk, but to expel him will demoralize our other cadets. I am at a loss for a resolution."

"Give him a starship," suggests the Sage.

"What? Have you not heard my concerns, or have you taken full loss of your faculties?" responds an incredulous Voice of Reason. "If I give James T. Kirk a starship he will be dead within two we . . . yes. Yes, I shall give him a starship. Excellent idea!"

"I thought you would like it."

As Cadet Kirk entered the Voice of Reason's chambers, he was not sure if he was receiving an award or being dismissed. It is always this way for the Adventurer. As he sat down to hear why he had been called to the office of the president of the Federation Council, he was not prepared for what he would hear.

"Congratulations, Cadet Kirk. We are giving you a starship," said the Voice of Reason.

"Whaaat? Shut the front door. Are you serious?" Kirk could barely contain his delight.

"Yes. We feel that your, um, innovative approach to solving problems makes you a wonderful candidate for commanding your own starship."

The newly appointed Captain Kirk was over the moon. As the news of his new commission began to sink in, Kirk's logical side turned to more strategic issues. "What is my mission?"

The Voice of Reason turned to look at the Sage. The Sage looks back blankly. Finally, the Sage speaks up, "Boldly go where no man has gone before."

"You mean just seek out new life and new civilizations?"

"Yep, exactly."

"Wow, that's kinda loose."

"We knew you'd like it." The Sage was feeling pretty good about how this was going.

"How long is my mission?" asked Captain Kirk. He wanted to get a sense of the Federation's commitment.

Again, the Voice of Reason turns to look at the Sage.

"Five years," responded the Sage, "maybe longer depending on how things go." The Sage whispered to the Voice of Reason, "He'll be dead in two weeks."

"Well, this is all very exciting. So, it's a five-year mission to explore strange new worlds, to seek out new life and new civilizations: to boldly go where no man has gone before. Do I have that right?"

"Yep, that's it."

"Do I need to call in from time to time?"

"Nope."

"Any policy manual I need to learn?"

"Nope, we figured you could wing it."

"I am *loving* this!"

"We thought you would." The Sage looked back at the Voice of Reason. "Well, Mr. President, I think we are done here. Captain Kirk, congratulations; you are free to go."

As Kirk rose and started to leave the office, the Voice of Reason whispered to the Sage, "What if he doesn't die right away? He is really talented. If he starts meddling with alien civilizations, he could alter the trajectory of entire universes!"

"No worries," replied the Sage. "Say, Captain Kirk, just one thing. It's not really a rule or a procedure; we know how you dislike those. Think of it as a directive—the one directive . . . the *prime* directive: Don't interfere in the natural development of alien civilizations. You okay with that? It really is nonnegotiable."

"Oh, I completely get that. Sure, no problem. Don't interfere with alien civilizations. Got it. Easy peasy lemon squeezy."

Now, what does Captain Kirk in virtually every episode of *Star Trek*? He kisses green women and kills lizard kings; he can't stop himself from interfering with alien civilizations. That's the Adventurer.

As leaders, Adventurers are natural entrepreneurs who inspire other with both a vision of a desired future state *and* a strategy for achieving it. They are less interested in the details and may be unaware of how others feel about this plan. They have a high risk tolerance, protecting against possible failure by logically thinking through the steps to achieve their goals. They value high performers and reward them with more responsibility and greater latitude.

As sales professionals, Adventurers are true hunters. They seek new markets, clients, and opportunities. They work best when given few parameters, thus allowing them to explore the "wilderness for fertile ground."

As service providers, Adventurers are creative problem solvers. They can be given challenging scenarios to troubleshoot and will be comfortable experimenting with new solutions. There is also the possibility that their risk taking will create different problems, but they will approach each situation with both innovation and logic.

As team members, Adventurers may prefer to work alone on unique projects. They enjoy being placed in novel situations and receiving great authority to work autonomously. Although they can and will work within an organizational structure, they also have a comfort with stretching the boundaries of the existing policies and procedures.

The swashbuckling Adventurer is another of Hollywood's favorites. Who doesn't like to follow the exploits of the fearless explorer through exotic locations, defending against unforeseen foes while pursuing some treasure? Errol Flynn, Harrison Ford as Indiana Jones, Angelina Jolie as Lara Croft, and Rachel Weisz in the *Mummy* movies have all portrayed this style. Harrison's Indiana Jones represents the prototypical Adventurer in his relentless pursuit of something valuable while also packing a whip, just in case.

Here's a quick reference guide for the Adventurer:

Role	Qualities
Leadership	• An inspiring visionary with a plan to achieve his or her goals • Direct communicator • Tends toward critical feedback • Rewards with additional responsibility and autonomy • Innovative and strategic • Less interested in details and morale
Sales Professional	• Comfortable in new markets • Assertive closer • Prefers loosely structured situations • Creatively matches client needs to products and services
Service Provider	• Innovative troubleshooter • Discovers unconventional fixes to customer service challenges • May work outside the boundaries to organizational policy • Willing to take chances to solve problems
Team Member	• Highly productive • Creative and logical • May prefer to work autonomously • Likes unusual assignments that allow for great latitude to operate

Chapter 4 Recognizing Each Style

The Behavioral Cues That Might Indicate Another Person's Style

Before we can begin to apply our knowledge of interactive styles, we must learn to recognize the behavioral cues that others provide us that alert us to their preference. We become much better leaders, sales professionals, service providers, colleagues, spouses, and friends when we can adjust successfully to other people's communication needs. And to do this, we must understand our own style as well as recognizing others'.

I suppose the easiest way to do this would be to give the other person the assessment. That might work for friends and family, perhaps even colleagues and team members, but handing your current or prospective customer an interactive style inventory to complete would be, well, odd—creepy, actually.

"Good morning, ma'am, and welcome to ABC Supply. Before I assist you, please complete this brief metacognitive assessment. The results will allow me to adjust my service approach to maximize your customer satisfaction. Ma'am? Ma'am? Where are you going? This is important! Really . . ."

Nope; that's just not going to work.

A better strategy is to develop your own cognitive schemas to recognize some of the telltale behavioral cues, both verbal and nonverbal. For the purposes of identifying style, we will focus only on the other person's preferred style—not the combination of primary and secondary preference that determines his or her Hollywood movie character. If you are able to correctly identify and adjust to this style, you will be successful within any scenario.

There are a couple things to remember about adjusting your style to another person's; for one thing, it will it require some effort. This effort may be a little uncomfortable, particularly at first. Sometimes it even feels stressful. If you recall from the Introduction of this book, the more effort (stress) we experience when adjusting to someone else, the more tempted we may be to label the other person as wrong or bad. That is not likely to be true, but it can feel that way. People who require less adjustment will feel easier, for sure. A Romantic working with a Romantic has to make very little adjustment and therefore expends little effort. In fact, you didn't even need to read this book to understand how to relate best with people who share the same preferred style as you.

Some level of effort will be expended when dealing with a style different from your own preferred style. For some people, there is very little effort expended; for others, a lot. It would be great if we all committed to expend the necessary effort to adjust to the other person's style, but that's simply not reasonable in all situations. If you'll recall, we *do* all have some level of intrinsic need to connect with one another; however, that motivation alone is not enough to push us through the effort necessary to connect. In social settings, both people are expected to adjust to achieve a comfortable rapport. If it is too difficult for one or both parties, then the consequence may simply be that the two of you don't hit it off. Oh well; there are 7 billion people on the planet. Not all of them will be your cup of tea.

But things are a little different in a professional context. More extrinsic pressures are involved. A leader's ability to build rapport and properly inspire performance out of his or her team will improve the organization and enhance the leader's reputation. It will also help the individual who is inspired. A sales professional's ability to build rapport with a potential client can lead to a sale, which has financial and career ramifications. A service provider who connects with a customer can build company loyalty, achieve higher customer satisfaction scores, and improve his or her professional standing. These extrinsic rewards can drive more effort toward adjusting to style.

I offer this caveat: On your own sheet you had a primary, secondary, tertiary, and quaternary preference. Adjusting to another person who uses your secondary style should be relatively easy. You simply need to learn how to recognize the behavioral cues and make that adjustment as quickly as possible. Adjusting to a person who uses your tertiary preference is more difficult. It requires both the ability to quickly identify the other person's style *and* adjust your approach in a way that is less comfortable for you. This takes sustained effort and repetition. You will become better over time, but you will also be exhausted afterward. Know this about yourself and manage your performance around it. For example, if you have a client who requires you to adjust to your tertiary preference, plan on having some down time afterward. If you can control your appointments and know your customers' styles, try to stagger those with preferences that differ from yours with those who have a similar style preference as you. This will keep your energy from being drained as the day goes on.

Now, for that last scenario we haven't discussed: The person with whom you are dealing has a preference for your quaternary style. In an ideal planet, where love and tolerance prevail, you would take a deep breath and dig deep into your toolbox of styles for that fourth tool. But we know that's not going to happen. I don't think it is reasonable to develop the interactive agility to go four tools deep, unless you have a very tight range on your distribution of preference (the 18–22 spread, compressed pattern). Rather than trying to use a style that is probably going to be clunky to execute and suck the lifeblood right out of you, I recommend that you identify a colleague who you find very irritating, introduce this person to your customer, and step away. They will probably love each other. Problem solved. The organization and customer are happy; you are not stressed out. Of course, this isn't always possible, but I still recommend this approach when you can use it.

HOW DO I RECOGNIZE ROMANTICS AND WARRIORS?

When looking for behavioral cues that indicate a person's preferred style, it is important to remember their intrinsic needs. For Romantics, that's appreciation. They love it when others praise them. They also like to do no harm to the emotional environment within which they find themselves. Remember, they are going for world peace. They want you to like them, and their behaviors generally support that desire for praise, unity, and likability. And the most universal nonverbal behavior to express a desire to be liked is the *smile*.

Romantics are the most naturally smiley of the four preferred styles. The smile indicates "I am friendly." The smile unifies people as allies, here to do no harm. That's not to say that Romantics are the *only* style that smiles; all styles will smile in certain situations. Romantics are more likely to style in more situations.

Romantics also like to focus on the person rather than the transaction. Even in professional situations, Romantics are more likely to use pleasantries, perhaps engage in small talk, and use the other person's name. I can often tell if I am dealing with a Romantic by that person's e-mails. Each contains a warm up, the point, and a cool down. It looks like this:

> Hey Dave!
> I hope you are having a great week. The summer weather patterns have arrived here in Orlando. Hot, humid, and thunderstorms every afternoon.

I can't believe that CLC is right around the corner. Crazy times around here, for sure. As we get closer to our event in August, I am putting the finishing touches on the planning. When you get a chance, can you send me an overview of your program so we can promote it on our website? I also need a head shot and bio for you as well. If you can get that to me by Friday, May 24, that would be great! Do you have any handouts that I can make copies for you? If so, please send them to me when you can and I will make copies for you. If you have any questions or need anything, please feel free to contact me by e-mail or on my mobile phone (226) 458–0115.

Have a great weekend and I look forward to seeing your presentation!:)

Chuck
Chuck Jackson
Event Planner
Personal Touch Events
"Where every event is a family affair!"

If Chuck were a Warrior, the e-mail would have read more like this:

Dave,
Please forward an overview of your program, a head shot, and bio to me by May 24.

THX,
Chuck
Chuck Jackson—Results Meetings
Sent from smartphone

As you can tell, the Romantic is willing to invest some time in personalizing the communication. This makes the person more likable. As we will learn later, the Warrior style is more interested in getting a result than being likable. In the Warrior's mind, this e-mail's purpose is to obtain an overview, photo, and bio, not to chat you up about the weather or how time flies. This same approach dominates the Warrior's in-person and phone conversations, too. The Warrior gets right to the point, often displaying a penetrating gaze and a furrowed brow rather than an inviting smile. These nonverbal behaviors are the product of a mind-set that wants to be efficient and productive. Oh, and don't forget to check out people's e-mail signatures. You will often find clues about their interactive style hidden there.

Romantics will ask you questions about you. This enhances the relationship. Often, in a shopping setting, Romantics are more people-focused than product-focused. They make eye contact with the staff and seek out a salesperson's assistance. Because people are the origin of emotion, Romantics are more likely to be compelled by the human element. Again, this is a very different strategy than the one used by Warriors.

Warriors' intrinsic need is *independence*. They rue being unnecessarily slowed by process, procedure, or people. Warriors generally enter a retail environment like they are on a recon-naissance mission. They walk with a purpose, even if they have no idea where they are going. They have exceptional foot speed. They make no direct eye contact with the staff until they have completed their data collection or when it has become obvious to them that they cannot find what they are looking for without help. Their biggest fear is being nabbed by an incompetent salesperson who will slow them down with unnecessary small talk, questions, and suggestions. Although Warriors appreciate high-value assistance, they are not willing to take their chances of having just *any* person waiting on them. For them, it is far better to get the lay of the land and to select the person who assists them rather than being the victim of a random staff member who approached them.

Here are some quick references to the verbal and nonverbal behavioral cues for Romantics:

- Have an easy smile
- Engage in small talk

- Are personable
- Take interest in you
- Are tactful and diplomatic
- Are most accessible (returns calls and e-mails)
- Make eye contact
- Seek assistance
- Use your name
- Are loyal
- Like consensus

Here are some quick references to the verbal and nonverbal behavioral cues for Warriors:

- Are direct
- Are intense
- Offer short answers
- Want to be "bottom lined"
- Are not interested in unnecessary details or stories
- Are a great source of referrals
- Value status and deals
- Are impatient/decisive
- Are competitive
- May display evidence of status (watch, car, clothes)

HOW DO I RECOGNIZE EXPERTS AND MASTERMINDS?

Experts tend to be very matter of fact. They convey seriousness in their interactions. Their questions (and they often have many) will be detailed and technical. They do not like to make mistakes and therefore strive to understand as much about a situation as possible. Remember, their intrinsic need is security. Using the retail store dynamic from the previous section, Experts may walk into the environment having already done research on the

Internet and/or in other stores. In fact, they may have printed material in their hand. They often ask for specific model numbers for the products that they are interested in. The store staff becomes a source of (hopefully) accurate information, and Experts then use them by asking many and detailed questions. Because they value as much data as possible, they may need time to analyze the information they collected, validate its accuracy, or compare it with other resources they have available. As a result, they make be very deliberate in their decision-making process.

If, in the aforementioned e-mail scenario, Chuck is an Expert, it may read like this:

Dear Conference Speakers,

As we near the dates of our annual Chapter Leadership Conference (CLC), it is important that we have all the necessary information to accurately depict your session content and personal qualifications. We plan to disseminate a CLC 2013 Agenda to all registered attendees on June 1, 2013. This agenda will contain a schedule of events, an overview of each session, a speaker biography, and a speaker photo. This information allows our attendees to best select the learning path they wish to pursue during the conference and maximizes the value of the experience.

In order to organize and publish this information by June 1, 2013, we require that all speakers complete the attached Program Overview Worksheet, being mindful to keep your word count to less than 300 words. The best overviews are brief but interesting and include three to five expected learning outcomes for the attendee. A sample overview from last year is also attached for your reference. Speaker biographies should be no longer than 200 words and will also serve as your introduction by one of our board members on the day of your presentation. Please focus on relevant job and educational experience rather than personal hobbies and data. Again, a sample and a worksheet for format have been provided. Finally, please send your head shot photo to us in a JPEG format.

All three of these documents are due on **Friday, May 24, 2013,** to ensure inclusion in our CLC 2013 Agenda. Failure to respond to this deadline may result in your seminar being poorly promoted at the event and greatly diminish attendance in your session. Also, because we are unable to accurately determine the exact number of attendees for each session, all handout copies will be the responsibility of the speaker. We recommend that you bring a minimum of 150 percent of the expected number of handouts to account for unexpected increases in participation. If you have any questions about the attached worksheets, samples, photo specifications, or attendance numbers, please contact Charles Jackson, Conference Planner, by phone or e-mail (details in the signature below).

Sincerely,

Charles Jackson, CMP

CLC Conference Planner
Applewood Event Management
3021 Duluth Street
Applewood, GA 40402
Office: (226) 956–2312
Mobile: (226) 458–0115
Fax: (226) 956–2320
E-mail: Charles.Jackson@CJEventManagement.com

Winner of the Industry Excellence Award 2005, 2007, 2008, 2009, 2011, 2012

If Charles is a Mastermind, the e-mail might go something like this:

> Greetings Mr. Dave!
> Looking forward to your session. I saw a video highlight on YouTube; what a crack up! Can we do a video to promote our session at CLC? I think it would be cool for people to get a taste of your style. We'd need to get it up fast, because registration begins pretty soon.
>
> Send me whatever information you have about the seminar and yourself so I can put that in the wampum we send to attendees. I'll need a photo, too. I'll probably be working on this next week, so no rush. When you get a chance drop me a line or give me a call about the thoughts on a video.
>
> *Jacks*
> C.A. Jackson
> Bedazzled Experiences
> "Innovative meetings for lasting impressions"
> Click **here** for a virtual tour of our new meeting planning on line assistant app.

The Masterminds' conceptual minds are easily distracted by the flashy aesthetic of great merchandising. They may have entered the retail store for no other reason than something caught their eye. Even if the store was an intended destination, they often become excited about products unrelated to the purpose of this visit. They are often enthusiastic and easily sidetracked. Masterminds' intrinsic need for excitement prompts them seek something new, different, and customizable to their life. For this reason, they are often drawn to things that are new, cool, and interesting, even if they don't need them. Their high-risk tolerance allows them to interact with products; they will turn things on, try out demos, twist knobs, and open doors.

Here are some quick references to the verbal and nonverbal behavioral cues for Experts:

- Are detailed and thorough
- Are educated (researched)
- Ask lots of questions
- Are conservative and serious
- Are risk avoidant
- Have a long sales cycle
- Are compliant to processes
- Take a technical/process approach
- Are respectful of procedures and politics

Here are some quick references to the verbal and nonverbal behavioral cues for Masterminds:

- Are creative
- Have systemic minds
- Bore easily
- Accept risk
- Like new, innovative, unconventional products, services, and ideas
- May go off in tangents during conversations
- May express their creativity in attire or accessories
- Have a short sales cycle
- Have an unusual approach

The key to recognizing any style is to pay close attention to both verbal and nonverbal cues. This means being very observant to others' patterns and, at least initially, asking more questions to let them talk. The more the other person talks, the more information you access to determine his or her interactive style.

I also find it helpful to use deductive reasoning to identify someone's style. For example, sometimes it is easier to *eliminate* a potential style than it is to identify it. Let's say I have an appointment to meet a prospective new client, someone whom I have never met before. When I walk into his office, I pay attention to his smile, his eye contact, how his office is decorated, and how he interacts with others. The friendlier and more casual a person appears, the more likely that he is neither a primary Expert nor Warrior. As I begin to get more information, perhaps he engages in small talk or inquires about topics that are unrelated to the purpose of this meeting; that confirms that I am dealing with either a Romantic or a Mastermind. Even if I can't determine the exact style, eliminating the preferences that this prospective client clearly does *not* use will help me better construct my message.

In the following chapters, we will examine exactly how to adjust your communication methods to each preferred style to be more effective as a leader, sales professional, service provider, colleague, family member, and friend.

Chapter 5 Leading Each Style

Creating a High-Performing Culture by Understanding Interactive Style

Leadership is hard. When I conduct classes on leadership, I often ask people to list the characteristics of an effective (not even great, just *effective*) leader. Here is a list of answers I received at a recent seminar when I asked a group of 50 people this simple question, "What makes a leader effective?"

Honesty	Confidence
Creativity	Trustworthiness
Fairness	Self-motivation
Consistency	Experience
Intelligence	Common sense
Drive	Loyalty
Passion	Productivity
Knowledge	Persuasiveness
Compassion	Resiliency
Accuracy	High moral standards

I then ask the group if they have ever met anyone who possessed *all* these attributes. Of course, the answer is no. Being a leader is hard, and others' expectations are enormously high. Add to that the fact that most people think the leader is omnipotent and that everything that happens within the leader's area of responsibility occurs with his or her full knowledge and intent, and you have to wonder why *anyone* would aspire to be a leader. It seems to be a thankless and near-impossible undertaking.

And yet, I call my company the Leadership Difference. Frequently, I am asked, "So what is the difference?" Well, I can't impeach the importance of any of the 20 items that my seminar group listed. All these qualities are vital and help a leader succeed. However, the one characteristic that I would list does not appear on this list. That quality is metacognition.

As I outlined in the Introduction, you may find many different definitions for *metacognition*. You'll recall that for my purposes, I consider metacognition to be the process of *thinking about how you think*. To me, great leaders have an incredible capacity to understand their own mind and to embrace other perspectives that allow them to broaden their own perception of situations. Great leaders also understand that they need to employ different strategies in different scenarios and with different types of people.

My first reaction when I listed those 20 attributes was, "There is no freaking way that any leader can possess all these." Eventually, it occurred to me that every person doesn't require every attribute from their leader. Certain types of people require certain types of behaviors from their leader to feel inspired. Let's look at this table again, but this time, we will assign each characteristic to the corresponding interactive style preference who would find that quality most appealing.

Appealing Leadership Qualities	Appeals Most to This Style
Trustworthiness	Romantic
Fairness	Romantic
Loyalty	Romantic
Compassion	Romantic
Honesty	Romantic
Confidence	Warrior
Common sense	Warrior
Drive	Warrior
Productivity	Warrior
Persuasiveness	Warrior
Consistency	Expert
Experience	Expert
Intelligence	Expert
Knowledge	Expert
Accuracy	Expert
Self-motivation	Mastermind
Passion	Mastermind
Resiliency	Mastermind
Enthusiasm	Mastermind
Creativity	Mastermind

By grouping the qualities by interactive style, we begin to see the keys to effectively leading each one. It also explains why a leader can be more effective with certain types of employees and struggle with others. One of the common phenomena I witness as I work with a broad and diverse client base is that many organizations develop a corporate culture. Corporate culture, by my definition, is when the employee population is dominated by a single interactive style. I have seen companies that are composed of more than 80 percent Romantics, for example. Sometimes this is reflective of the industry they are in (hospitality, for example, attracts Romantics because of the service excellence dynamic, whereas Experts may be nearly ubiquitous at an engineering firm).

But there is another reason this organizational development phenomenon can occur: Leaders often hire people who think like they do. This is a very dangerous practice that can result in a highly myopic organization. It is understandable how this could happen, given that strong corporate cultures often contribute to high morale, good communication, and low turnover. It is an easy environment within which to lead. However, the performance potential of these homogeneous organizations is often hamstrung by their narrow view. They're rarely serving a market that lacks the diversity of their own company. As a result, these organizations are often out of step with market demands and fail to thrive.

Leaders who aspire to create a diverse organization that is more heterogeneous in its style composition will certainly be more challenged. They will continually need to engage in metacognition to determine the correct strategies to inspire high levels of performance, enhance communication, and keep morale high. They will have to work harder to build consensus. The reward, though, is a much higher level of potential performance and an organization that more closely reflects the market that they serve.

One of the most important keys to effectively leading this diverse work environment is reflected in those attributes listed earlier. Motivation is fundamental to employee performance—and essential to motivation is the fulfillment of intrinsic needs. Let's restructure those attributes that represent an effective leader one more time. But this time, we'll include each interactive style's intrinsic need.

Romantic	**Intrinsic Need: Appreciation**
	Relationships built on likability
	Values honesty
	Values fairness
	Values compassion
	Values trustworthiness
	Values loyalty
	Responds best to a leader who cares about him or her and takes a personal interest in his or her life, both professionally and personally
Mastermind	**Intrinsic Need: Excitement**
	Relationships built on new and different
	Values creativity
	Values passion
	Values self-motivation
	Values resiliency
	Values enthusiasm
	Responds best to a leader who is open to and considers his or her ideas and who also assigns new and special projects from time to time
Expert	**Intrinsic Need: Security**
	Relationships built on dependability
	Values consistency
	Values intelligence
	Values knowledge

(*continued*)

(*continued*)

	Values accuracy Values experience Responds best to a leader who provides thorough training and a well-designed work structure and who consistently applies policies and procedures
Warrior	**Intrinsic Need: Independence** Relationships built on efficiency Values drive Values confidence Values common sense Values productivity Values persuasiveness Responds best to a leader who provides clear goals and allows the freedom to pursue results without excessive management

Notice that I added a summary statement at the end of each interactive style's section that begins with "Responds best to a leader who . . ." This is the bottom line. The best leaders can adjust their approach based on the needs of their associate. A single employee doesn't need you to possess all 20 of those characteristics in *each interaction*. What employees desire is that they are experiencing leadership that *best coaxes maximum performance* from them. That requires leaders to engage in metacognition, choosing the motivational strategy that works best for the individual(s) involved.

COACHING AND COUNSELING BY STYLE

There are a few nuances related to each style that affect the effectiveness of coaching and counseling. As discussed earlier,

Romantics require the occasional venting session to empty their CTL container. If the leader does not provide this outlet, the alternative can often be toxic. Romantics may interpret their leader's unwillingness to allow them to vent as evidence that he or she doesn't care about them, which is very demotivational to Romantics. They will seek other outlets, often fellow team members, and add their leader to the list of "crap" in their container.

Romantic leaders understand the value of venting. However, the other three interactive styles—particularly the Warrior— may not. It is important for all leaders to recognize the role venting plays in Romantics' performance. It's like preventive maintenance. Anyone who has a car makes a choice about how to handle routine oil changes. One strategy is to change the oil at regular intervals even though the car seems to be performing just fine. The other strategy is to drive the car until it starts to make a funny noise and smell bad. Unfortunately, the car never performs quite as well. The same could be said about people. As a leader, you can provide a consistent, regularly scheduled opportunity for people to vent any frustrations, or you can wait until the employee starts to make a funny noise and smell bad (metaphorically, hopefully). In the latter scenario, the employee never performs quite as well again.

One technique that I have had success with personally is people preventive maintenance sessions (PPMS). Yes, the acronym is not lost on me. This is not a style-specific (or gender-specific, for that matter) issue; *all* employees respond well to PPMS. Here's how it works, step by step:

- Each month, schedule a 15- to 30-minute meeting with each team member.
- *Execute these meetings casually* (over a cup of coffee, not in your office), but *track them formally* to ensure that you speak with each team member every month.
- Make sure the conversation is driven by the employee, not you.

- Ask these questions or some variation:
  ○ What is on your mind related to work issues?
  ○ What would help you perform your job even better?
  ○ How can I be a better leader for you?
  ○ Is there anything else on your mind that you want to talk about?
- Be sure to follow up on any issues that your employees discussed during the meeting.
- Expect the first few meetings to go very fast and include very little information. By about the third meeting, the team members will become more comfortable with the idea and begin sharing more.

This approach provides a consistent, enduring vehicle for team members to provide you with feedback, vent any concerns, share their ideas, and discuss any needs for more information or training. Essentially, it allows each of the four interactive styles to get their intrinsic needs fulfilled. And remember, when employees' intrinsic needs are fulfilled, they perform at their highest level.

PROGRESSIVE COUNSELING

Counseling is not my favorite part of being a leader. I am sure that's because I'm a Romantic. As a servant leader whose corporate motto is "to positively affect the life of each person with whom we come in contact," the whole prospect of sitting down with someone and pointing out aspects of his or her performance that are not meeting standards is very unappealing. Logically (and I am a secondary Warrior), I understand that I actually *am* helping the person by pointing out what needs to be done to improve, but emotionally, it just feels crummy.

To feel more comfortable with the counseling process, I devised an approach that outlines the accountability for both leader and team member as it relates to the steps of progressive counseling. For clarity, here is how I define *progressive counseling*:

- *Verbal counseling:* This is the initial conversation between leader and team member to correct a behavior that reflects substandard performance relative to the clearly articulated expectations or a minor policy violation.
- *Written warning:* This reflects a second conversation related to performance deficiencies as measured by actual results compared to clearly articulated goals or expectation. This could also be a second violation of a policy or a more serious first policy violation.
- *Final warning:* This conversation represents the notification of the team member that substandard performance will result in termination if not corrected in a very specific time frame. Final warning can also be administered for numerous violations of the same minor policy or for a violation of a serious policy such as a standard of conduct issue.
- *Termination:* In the words of Donald Trump, "You're fired!"

In my opinion, counseling revolves around troubleshooting two important questions:

- Is the team member able to perform at the required level or comply with the existing policy?
  - If no, will further training provide the team member with the adequate skills to perform and/or comply?
    - If yes, make arrangements for additional training.
    - If no, examine the hiring process to determine how an individual who is unable to perform and/or comply within the parameters of this job was hired.
  - If yes, then the team member must be unwilling; see next question.
- Is the team member willing to perform at the required level or comply with the existing policy?

○ If yes, then the team member must be unable to perform or comply; see previous question.

○ If no, is there a motivational factor missing in the environment that can be corrected to change the person's willingness?
Romantics = more appreciation
Warriors = more independence
Experts = more security
Masterminds = more excitement

- If yes, the leader can strive to introduce more of this intrinsic reward.

- If no and it is deemed that the employee is unwilling to perform at the required level or comply with existing policy and there are adequate intrinsic rewards in the environment, progressive counseling will be continued.

So, using my model for progressive counseling combined with the troubleshooting approach, I arrived at this philosophy for executing progressive counseling.

Verbal counseling lays the accountability for the performance or policy compliance deficiency squarely on the leader. This conversation acknowledges that the employee must need additional training or motivation to meet the job's requirements; otherwise, the person has been hired for a position he or she is not qualified to fulfill. In all three of these scenarios, the leader is responsible for providing a solution.

Written warning provides a shared accountability between the leader and team member. It is during this conversation that the leader can address the previous interventions (additional training, motivational elements, etc.) that have been attempted to achieve the expected behaviors. Although the leader continues to be responsible for correcting the current deficiency, the team member also has responsibility to meet expectations.

The final warning completes the shift of accountability from the leader to the team member. At this point, it should be very clear that the leader has provided adequate training and motivation and that the only person who can successfully achieve the expected results is the team member. A specific time frame should be provided in which the team member must accomplish these expectations. If the team member fails to reach the required level of performance or compliance within that time frame, the consequence will be termination.

This sliding accountability—leader, leader/team member, team member—works well for all interactive styles, both as a leader and as a team member. It helps Romantic leaders approach progressive counseling in a manner that seems more positive emotionally and helps them feel less guilty for holding others accountable. For Warrior leaders, it can soften the initial counseling steps and allow for the greatest likelihood of achieving the most appealing outcome: the team member's improvement. It provides Expert leaders with a clear process to follow, thereby ensuring that they can navigate a conceptual aspect of their job in a secure way. And it gives Mastermind leaders a structure for improving their team's performance, thereby helping them remain consistent in their approach to team member counseling.

THINGS TO CONSIDER WHEN COUNSELING EACH STYLE

Of course, the leader's style is only half of the consideration when delivering a counseling session. The interactive style of the team member receiving the counseling may affect how that person responds. Most individuals do not enjoy criticism, even if it is constructive and well delivered. *Well-delivered counseling* means that the leader:

- Schedules the meeting in a private location.
- Has a genuine desire for the team member to improve.
- Holds a direct, to-the-point conversation.
- Offers fact-based and detailed information (no hearsay).
- Is open to solutions offered by the team member.

However, even when all these elements exist, some toxic behaviors can emerge. Many of these behaviors can be associated with the team member's interactive style. Here are a few you might anticipate.

Romantics

Because both criticism and conflict are generally uncomfortable for Romantics, they often react in more emotionally charged ways. They may be extremely apologetic or become defensive and angry. They may even cry. It is very important that the leader take a supportive position with the Romantic team member and explain his or her commitment to helping the Romantic improve in ability to perform and/or comply effectively. This is a good time to allow the Romantic to vent frustrations about the job if needed—so long as the Romantic makes specific behavioral commitments to correct the current performance deficiencies at the conclusion of the venting. If a leader doesn't allow a Romantic to vent, the team member will likely pursue another, less productive outlet for his or her feelings—one that often involves other team members and the employee break room.

Warriors

Warrior team members are more comfortable having a direct confrontation and as such may argue the validity of your opinion. If they do not agree that their performance is deficient or if they fail to see the value of policy compliance, they will likely tell you. This can lead to an uncomfortable verbal sparring. In fact, because Warriors often believe that the "end justifies the means," they will point to their results as evidence that their approach, despite its potential negative collateral impact, is working just fine.

I believe it is always useful to listen to the perspective of another, even in a progressive counseling dynamic. However, a protracted argument is neither productive nor conducive to fixing the current performance concern. At some point, it is necessary for the leader to remind the team member that it is the *leader's* responsibility to assess each individual's performance contribution and provide feedback. This responsibility is often subjective in nature, but that doesn't change the fact that it is *solely the leader's* responsibility. If the Warrior disagrees with the leader's assessment, he or she is welcome to attach a document for the employee file that explains the team member's position. As for the progressive counseling, that will not be changed.

Experts

It is essential that you have all your facts straight and data prepared to support your position *before* you counsel Experts. Remember, they hate mistakes—and a counseling session represents a mistake on steroids. They are very likely to dig their heels in and deny that they are not performing correctly; they will defend themselves strongly with evidence of improper training, poor communication, or inconsistent expectations from the leader that are responsible for the situation, rather than their own efforts. They will likely point to others' performance as proof that their own situation is no different—and maybe even worse—than others who do not seem to be under fire. Even after the counseling session, Experts may continue to plead their case by bringing more evidence to the leader. It is wise for the leader to offer a very specific, detailed plan of communication, training, and feedback to Expert team members to ensure that they fully understand what is expected and have received ample support to meet these requirements.

Masterminds

No one is more surprised by progressive counseling than the Mastermind. Masterminds were completely unaware that they were not performing adequately. As I often say, Warriors write the rules to keep others working effectively (they just don't always follow them). Romantics communicate the rules to make sure everyone is comfortable with them. Experts follow the rules and point out when others don't. And Masterminds have no idea there are rules. And once they're aware of the rules, they consider their situation to be an exception.

Delivering progressive counseling can be very demotivating to a Mastermind. You must remain optimistic and express confidence that this situation can be improved but also be very specific about the behaviors that you need changed and the time frame within which this must happen. Follow up with the Mastermind at regular intervals to ensure that the counseling isn't being dismissed or interpreted in unintended ways.

* * *

Leadership is a complicated concept. It differs from management. In my mind, leadership is essentially the ability to achieve the desired results using the skills and talents of a diverse group of people while maintaining a positive environment that ensures a sustainable effort in the future. Management is the collection of all the other responsibilities that are ancillary to the leadership responsibilities. If you can effectively inspire, coach, and counsel all team member styles, you are well on your way to becoming an exceptional leader.

Chapter 6 Selling to Each Style

You Can Expand Your Market Share by Adjusting to Your Consumer's Interactive Style

I prefer to take a collaborative and consultative approach to sales. This is consistent with our corporate mission "to positively affect the life of each person with whom we come in contact." It is also aligned with my Romantic/Warrior (Crusader) interactive style. I had always approached selling by first understanding my clients' needs and *then* developing an approach to address those challenges. However, it wasn't until I was hired by a luxury consumer appliance manufacturer that I developed a detailed model for *consultative selling*. The impetus for that design was the result of a visit I made to the client's manufacturing facility and learning center. Management had heard of my work with another organization and asked if I could meet them at their central location.

When I arrived at their facility, I was immediately impressed by the quality of the experience. The executive vice president (EVP) met me and offered to begin our meeting with a tour of their education center. The EVP was a tall, lean, and proper man. He exuded an air of grace and intelligence. He also reflected a certain stoicism that told me he was a man of no nonsense. I immediately had him pegged as the Sage (Warrior/Expert). We began the tour after brief pleasantries. From that moment on, in keeping with the style of the Sage, he shared information of a strictly factual nature.

Their learning center was as amazing as I have ever seen. The lobby area was adorned with breathtaking art—clearly the result of the work of a talented interior decorator. The primary training venue bore a greater resemblance to a Broadway theater than to a classroom. Comfy chairs with armrests and optional foldout writing tables arose at an angle from the stage to the audiovisual booth. And the stage, oh my! It was straight out of the performing arts, complete with curtain and a middle section that could be dropped using hydraulics to replace displays. Oh, and it also could rotate to reveal previously hidden displays to the audience. It was *stunning*.

We moved upstairs to an area that had been designed to showcase their product line. Some of the nation's finest home designers had developed individual kitchen vignettes to highlight the luxury appliances. Having grown up working in my father's small town appliance store, I had a tremendous appreciation for how magnificent these displays were. All of it was truly breathtaking—none more than one particular refrigerator, the top of their line. As we approached the appliance, the EVP visibly puffed with pride. He started running down the engineering and aesthetic marvels that were all contained within this one unit. It was clear that he felt for this refrigerator much like it was his own child. When he finished, I asked, "How much does something like this cost?"

"$14,000," he replied casually.

"$14,000! Does it come with sexual favors?"

(I really need to work on my tendency to blurt things out.)

The EVP didn't respond. In retrospect, if this appliance was like a daughter to him, I'm pretty sure my weak attempt at humor was very inappropriate—especially to a Sage, let alone a prospective client. Still, we continued the tour and ended at the EVP's office.

"Well, you certainly have an impressive product line, and your commitment to training is evident in the quality of this facility. What I'd like to better understand is what your training needs are and see if I am a good match for helping you achieve those."

The reply? "Our dealers are struggling with price objections."

My internal warrior wanted so badly to say, "Um, ya think?! Here's a thought: Stop selling *$14,000* refrigerators. I mean, my dad had a side-by-side refrigerator with water and ice in the door at the front of his store for five years because it cost $699. Who the hell spends that much money on a refrigerator?" For once, however, my Romantic side prevailed.

"I see. Well, I think I can help with that. If we teach the dealers to use a consultative approach to selling, they can become more familiar with their clients' specific needs as well as their interactive styles. This will allow your dealers to better frame your product line to maximize the appliance's appeal, increase its perceived value, and ensure that the story they tell about your products truly resonates with the consumer in front of them. Plus, it will help them anticipate specific objections and address them early in the sales process. Furthermore, I can give them a model that is designed solely to help ease price sensitivity."

And the Sage smiled.

For the next three years, I traveled the country helping dealers better understand the luxury consumer. They learned to identify different interactive styles' behavioral cues, as well as how to adjust their sales approach to better appeal to each. In essence, they learned to communicate the value of these luxury appliances in a way that their customers truly understood, allowing them to experience the value of the product instead of being negatively influenced by a poorly matched sales delivery. Basically, I viewed these appliances much like the works of art featured in the company headquarters' lobby. It is art at the highest level: art of incredible beauty and value. Unfortunately, if you put this art in the wrong frame, the buyer doesn't see the beauty and value; instead, the buyer gets caught up in the frame. My job, therefore, was framing.

This chapter will explore my model of consultative selling. We will examine how each style requires a different approach to relationship building and product framing. We'll also consider the negotiation techniques each style uses, as well as common objections—and a model for addressing them.

For the purposes of our discussion, Figure 6.1 outlines the steps of the consultative sales process.

Let's look at each of these in detail.

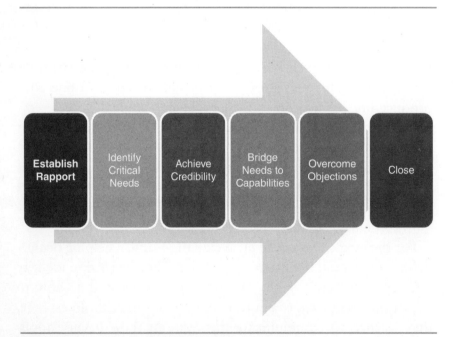

FIGURE 6.1 Consultative Sales Process

ESTABLISH RAPPORT

Teddy Roosevelt is credited with saying, "Nobody cares how much you know until they know how much you care." This is never as true as during the sales process. Every consumer wants a sales professional who understands how he or she likes to experience shopping. The right sales professional adds value to the products and services, because he or she recognizes the best way to treat the consumer and how to highlight the offerings. Even talented sales professionals can impede the process if they deliver their service in a way that the consumer doesn't appreciate. When sales professionals focus on product features that are unimportant to the consumer, they have essentially, to paraphrase Peter Drucker, done something well that need not be done at all. Failing to effectively develop rapport with the customer is the surest way to failure. Sure, there are those customers who are so motivated to purchase a product that they are willing to step over the carnage that is your rapport building skills. But I don't think you can bet on that demographic to get you through your career.

Each interactive style prefers the salesperson to take a specific approach to rapport building. The basis of the relationship is an extension of the intrinsic needs of the individuals. Because Romantics' intrinsic need is appreciation, they want to deal with a likable sales professional. This means someone who treats them like a person, not a transaction. They respond to someone who displays a genuine smile, learns and uses their name in a sincere manner, and takes a personal interest in them. It is important for the salesperson to ask lots of questions to truly understand the lifestyle of Romantics. Do they have kids? Have they lived in this area long? What kinds of things do they like most about their current product? What do they not like?

It is also very useful for sales professionals to find some common elements in their lives. Identifying the similarities between the Romantic consumer and the sales professional helps build empathy and creates a stronger relationship. Having a relationship with the sales professional is critical to the Romantic consumer. That's why Romantics are the most people-focused consumers during the sales process. They want to know they can trust the person they are working with.

Warrior consumers are much less interested in the relationship they have with their salesperson—and far more concerned with efficiency. Because their intrinsic need is independence, they may not even accept the initial offer of service the sales professional makes. They expect that a sales professional will be able to quickly identify their critical needs, match those needs to the right product/service, and then be ready to negotiate aggressively.

I find that Warrior consumers are the easier to sell to (at least until the closing/negotiation step). They don't want to waste time, and they are the least likely to shop around. If they have begun the sales process with you, they really want this to go well. That means they want to work with sales professionals who know what they are doing, can quickly match their situation to the product's features, and can succinctly articulate the value logically. They also want sales professionals who have the authority to negotiate the price and terms without unnecessary delay or red tape. Whereas engaging in small talk and learning the lifestyle context is critical to a Romantic consumer, it is actually very irritating to the Warrior customer. Questions should be quickly funneled from open ended to close ended, and options should be pared down rapidly. Again, the bulk of the time the Warrior is willing to invest will be in negotiating a better deal.

Expert consumers hate being or feeling stupid. As mentioned in Chapter 4 on recognizing each style, they often do research before engaging a sales professional and then use the sales professional as resource to answer the many questions they've devised. This can feel like an inquisition as the questions get increasingly more detailed and technical. The purpose of the inquisition is only partially educational; it is also a test of trustworthiness. At some point the questions seem to extend beyond what a consumer would need to know. In fact, they may be so detailed that answers don't even matter—because they don't affect the value of the product or service. This is a dangerous moment for the sales professional. Here's how that may go (and I have abbreviated the inquisition—believe me).

Expert: So, this is the DX345, right?

Salesperson: Yes, it is.

Expert: This has a self-cleaning oven feature, right?

Salesperson: Yes, it does.

Expert: It's my understanding that you do not need to add any cleaner, correct?

Salesperson: No, it cleans by heat alone.

Expert: What temperature does the oven reach during the self-cleaning process.

Salesperson: I believe it is in excess of 800 degrees.

Expert: From what I have read, more like 900 to 1,000 degrees.

Salesperson *(under breath)*: Which is in excess of 800 degrees.

Expert: I understand that the self-cleaning process can actually damage the oven.

Salesperson: I haven't heard that.

Expert: Yep. The extreme temperature can damage the fuse and blow out the control panel. Pretty expensive to fix, I hear.

Salesperson: I'm not aware of any of those problems.

Expert: There are several stories about it on the Internet. Do you know how the manufacturer has engineered this oven to avoid that?

The next response from the sales professional will be very important. The best way to handle this may seem counter-intuitive. The answer should be:

Salesperson: I don't know. I have been selling these appliances for x years, and no one has ever asked

> me that. That's a great question. No one here knows
> more about these cooking appliances than me. I'll need
> to call the manufacturer.

You can offer to find out if it is truly important to the Expert consumer, but my bet is the consumer doesn't really need to know the answer. What the Expert really wanted to know is *if your other answers could be trusted*. By confessing that *you don't know* the answer to this question, you have validated your answers to the other questions—because you proved that you are willing to admit when you don't know something. In addition, the fact that you admit you are stumped tickles the Expert consumer. That's a story the consumer can tell for many years to come. The Expert will buy the oven just because of that! Let the consumer win. The Expert spent all that time on research and wants to share it.

Now, it *is* important that you *establish credibility* before saying, "I don't know." This exchange would be much less effective:

Expert: So this is the DX345, right?

Salesperson: I don't know. That's a great question. I'll need to call the manufacturer.

Too quick. You don't even know what product you're selling? Yikes.

Masterminds like what is unique, cool, and innovative. They may have entered your place of business for a specific purpose, but it's not because they've done research on what you're offering. They likely saw a creative advertisement or an eye-catching window display. Once inside your location, they may be distracted by things that are more interesting than what originally drew them in. They love to work with sales professionals who are enthusiastic and excited about the products and services they sell. They may go off on tangents while explaining what brought them to the store that day. If in a retail setting,

Masterminds may run a sales professional all around the store in a whirlwind. It is both thrilling and potentially maddening. The important thing is to indulge their ideas and appeal to their creativity. Slowly eliminate options and get them focused on specific products or solutions. Be sure to close aggressively and not let them leave your business without a commitment. Otherwise, you may experience this scenario:

Mastermind: Oh my God. I *love* this living room decor. Let me go home and take some measurements and then I will call you to make delivery arrangements. Oh my God. I am so excited and *so* glad I stopped in. To think, I was only looking for a lamp, and now I am getting a whole new living room!

Salesperson: It's a very cool decor. You're going to love it. So you'll call me tomorrow?

Mastermind: Yes. Let me just confirm everything and check my schedule. I'll call you later.

(Three days pass. The salesperson calls the Mastermind.)

Salesperson: Hey, Mastermind, this is your salesperson at Ultra Cool Furnishings. I just wanted to schedule that delivery.

Mastermind: Who?

Salesperson *(slightly alarmed)*: The salesperson at Ultra Cool Furnishings. Remember? You were here on Monday and loved the living room decor we picked out. You were going to call me to set up a delivery.

Mastermind: *Oh, right!* Ultra Cool Furnishings. Hey, man! I bought a boat.

(Sad trombone sound effect.)

To avoid this disappointing loss of a sale, the salesperson should have obtained some form of financial commitment from the Mastermind during that initial interest. Simply by taking a deposit, the Mastermind would have made a solid commitment during the store visit and not continued to explore other options. Unfortunately, leaving the store without making a commitment, the Mastermind was free to continue shopping—for a boat. No solution is foolproof, of course, and the Mastermind may still have gone a radically different direction. But the deposit would have at least given the salesperson greater leverage in closing this sale.

FRAMING TIPS

You might be asking yourself, "What do I mean by *framing*?" Here's how I describe the concept of framing your product or service. As discussed at the beginning to this chapter, a piece of art's appeal and quality is very important when you decide to purchase a painting. After all, the value of the work is the *art*, not the frame. Unfortunately, even a beautiful piece of art that appeals directly to your taste will suffer if it is in a bad frame. If the frame doesn't reflect your home decor, then the art loses value. As a result, a mismatched frame can cause even the finest painting to be overlooked.

Selling your products and services has the same challenge. Even if you're selling something that's *perfect* for the customer, you are essentially putting the art in the wrong frame if you explain the value in an incorrect way. Of course, there is no *one* incorrect way; it depends on the style of the person to whom you're selling. If you fail to represent your products in a manner that makes sense to the consumer, then you are diminishing the value of your products. Consultative selling requires that you correctly match consumers' needs to your products *and* explain that value in a way that resonates with them. Poor framing is a more common reason for not closing a sale than the product or service itself.

Romantics tend to spend more for others than they do for themselves. Once you have clearly identified a Romantic's needs, imagine how the appropriate product or service would benefit the Romantic consumer's *family and friends*. As you discuss its appropriate features, focus on the value these features would have on the loved ones of the Romantic customer. This frame appeals to the Romantic's intrinsic need for appreciation and to be liked.

Warriors, on the other hand, are comfortable with status. They recognize the value of performance and brand recognition. Because they are generally competitive in nature, having a product that is associated with "best of breed" is like having a trophy. By framing a product's superiority, its reputation, and the iconic nature of the brand, you appeal to the Warrior's sense of independence and competitiveness. Just be ready to negotiate, because the Warrior also wants to win at the register! The bottom line for Warriors is to remember that they are not afraid to display their success; therefore, you should frame products and services to highlight how they underscore this attribute. Warriors are also logical, so establishing how your offering will add value to their life is powerful.

Experts respond best if the product has a well-known history of craftsmanship, reliability, and quality. By focusing on the product or service's heritage and its well-known reputation as a dependable and safe choice, you appeal to Experts' desire for security and avoidance of risk. After all, Experts don't do all that online research for nothing. By focusing on your offering's unimpeachable tradition of quality, you reinforce for Experts that the decision to purchase this is beyond reproach.

Masterminds want a lifestyle that differs from others', one that is unique and exciting. They're much more attracted to products and services that offer alternatives to the conventional experience. A successful framing effort by the sales professional would emphasize the unusual or cutting-edge features that appeal to a trend-setting and alpha consumer like the Mastermind.

I have used these techniques with clients in a variety of industries. Let me give you an example of framing using common kitchen appliances, because this is an item that all of us are familiar with as consumers. Imagine a customer has entered a showroom to purchase new appliances for the kitchen. Let's consider how each interactive style would prefer the sales process proceed.

The Romantic enters the store and, wanting to make a human connection, immediately looks around for the sales staff. She makes eye contact with the individual who approaches her and greets that person with a smile, an introduction, and a hand-shake. The salesperson reciprocates. The sales professional and Romantic engage in some small talk and casually begin to explore the reason for the visit to the showroom.

Salesperson: So, what brings you into our showroom today?

Jennifer (Romantic): Well, I'm thinking about updating my kitchen appliances. My current appliances are fine, but they are getting a little long in the tooth, you know? They actually came with the house when we bought it 10 years ago, and they look a little dated. Plus, our family has grown, and I have become a bit more committed to cooking—so I feel like the appliances haven't really kept up. You know what I mean?

Salesperson: Absolutely, Jennifer. There have been so many advances made in the features of refrigerators and cooking appliances over the past 10 years. The food preservation and energy efficiency features alone in refrigerators can help you stretch the family food budget and save money on utilities. Do you keep leftovers?

Jennifer: Yes, I try to make sure we get at least two meals out of a dinner. Both my husband and I work, so when I have time to cook a meal it is important for us to be able to get the most out of that meal!

Salesperson: Oh, what do you and your husband do for a living?

Jennifer: My husband is a contractor, and I am a pharmacist.

Salesperson: Yes, I can see where time would be precious. Those are very demanding jobs. It sounds like you have children, too, based on your comment that your family is growing?

Jennifer: Yes, we have two: a boy and a girl. The boy is eight, and the girl is five.

Salesperson: That's fantastic. I have two kids, too. They are much older than yours, but I can appreciate how busy it must be to have kids that age with both you and your husband working. The reason I ask is that one of the qualities you may want to focus on in a refrigerator is the air filtration system. The reason food spoils faster in some refrigerators than in others has a lot to do with the way the air is circulated and filtered. The best systems for maintaining clean air with appropriate levels of humidity will allow you to store food for much longer. This will help you keep your leftovers, and all your food for that matter, fresh for a longer period of time. That way your family can experience better-tasting meals and you can reduce the cost of spoilage.

Jennifer: I hadn't even thought of that. What a great way of thinking about the refrigerator! *(Jennifer has grown increasingly happy about her choice of salesperson. He really understands her needs.)*

Salesperson: Yes. I think most of us, including me at one time, think of the refrigerator as something that keeps things cold. The reality is the refrigerator's job is to store and preserve food. The better it does that, the more value it provides our family. Now, let's talk about how you like to prepare meals for your family. You said you have become more committed to cooking; tell me about that.

In this example, the salesperson invested time in *getting to know the Romantic*. He displayed likability by engaging in small talk, using the Romantic's name, and asking questions to learn about Jennifer's lifestyle and family. He also displayed empathy for her situation by pointing out the similarities in their lives. Relationships are often built on common experiences, and the sales professional was quick to align their backgrounds, pointing out that they both have dealt with raising children and expressing an admiration of parenting while navigating a demanding career. He then framed the refrigerator's features by highlighting the features that will have a value to her family, a very appealing benefit to a Romantic because it prompts *others to appreciate her efforts.*

Now, had Jennifer been a Warrior, a very different scenario would unfold:

Jennifer enters the showroom at a quick and determined pace, avoiding eye contact with the sales staff. She moves quickly to the area of the showroom that contains the appliances in which she is interested. The sales professional approaches.

Salesperson: Good morning. What brings you into our show-room today?

Jennifer (Warrior): I am looking for new kitchen appliances.

Salesperson: I see, are we talking about both refrigerators and cooking appliances?

Jennifer: Yes. *(Jennifer checks her e-mail on her phone.)*

Salesperson: Okay. What is most important to you when evaluating appliances?

Jennifer: I don't really know, frankly. I just know mine look like crap.

Salesperson *(laughs)*: How old are your current appliances?

Jennifer: I'm not sure. They came with the house. Probably more than 15 years old.

Salesperson: Yes, it's probably time to shop then. There have been lots of changes since then. The kitchen has become the focal point of the house. In fact, upgrading your kitchen really enhances your home, not just aesthetically but also in resale value. There are brands on the market that have such a reputation that their mere existence in your house makes a statement. Are you familiar with this line? *(The salesperson directs Jennifer to a luxury product line.)*

Jennifer: Actually, I am. I was at a party at a physician's house this past Christmas, and she has this type of refrigerator.

Salesperson: Well, this is about as good as it gets. The technology and design are considered the best out there.

Jennifer: Yeah, and the price is, too!

Salesperson *(laughs)*: Yeah, they ain't cheap. The best never are. However, when you have a statement like this in your kitchen, your resale value immediately goes up. Plus, if you are looking to create a kitchen that looks amazing—that is impressive rather than crap—this is the kind of product line that wows people.

Jennifer: It is sharp. Why does it cost so much money?

Salesperson: Well, you are buying a product that's renowned for being the best in the world. Just like with cars, clothes, and jewelry, appliances have a pecking order. This product line is at the top. All the other products aspire to achieve a position in the market that this line inhabits. Owning this appliance basically says you possess the best. Plus, it adds value to your home when you have this appliance in your kitchen.

Jennifer: Hmm, I like that. *(Jennifer checks her voice mail while continuing to engage with the salesperson.)*

Notice the differences in this exchange. The Warrior uses nonverbal behaviors to avoid immediate service. Rather than opening with a question that can be answered "no"—such as, "May I help you?"—the sales professional asks an open-ended question. Warrior Jennifer's response is short and sweet, not the expanded answer that Romantic Jennifer provided—another indication that we are dealing with a Warrior. During the conversation, Warrior Jen is multitasking (checking e-mail and voice mail). This isn't a "squirrel moment" from a Mastermind but rather a way to maximize productivity—a common trait of Warriors. The fact that Warrior Jennifer knows her appliances look like crap indicates that she is aware of how her kitchen compares with others' (especially her physician friend's), and it is not favorable. The salesperson adeptly steers Warrior

Jennifer toward the appliances that have the greatest cachet, knowing that an impressive product line that's recognizable for its place in the space will appeal to her. He even goes so far as to point out that this product line is a "winner," a quality that very much appeals to Warrior Jennifer. Finally, using the logic that enhancing the kitchen actually increases the value of the home is a very compelling argument for the logical Warrior.

Whereas Warriors desire an efficient, outcome-oriented shopping experience, Experts want to ensure that their purchase decision is well researched and above reproach in terms of judgment and quality. Let's consider this encounter:

An Expert walks in carrying a copy of *Consumer Reports* and a stack of printed Internet pages. He scans the showroom to understand the layout. He slowly makes his way to the area of the store that features the specific appliances he has researched. The sales professional approaches.

Salesperson: Good morning. I noticed you walked specifically over to this product line.

Dan (Expert): Yes, I am renovating my kitchen and am interested in learning more about the Delvon appliances. Is this the BOV123?

Salesperson: Yes, it is. Good eye. You clearly know your stuff. What is it about the Delvon appliances that appeal to you?

Dan: Well, according to *Consumer Reports*, this is the most reliable appliance line on the market. They also offer the longest warranty. One thing that concerns me, however, is that this model says BOV123S. The *Consumer Reports* review didn't list the S.

Salesperson: The S is simply a color designation. This refrigerator comes in white, black, and stainless steel.

Dan *(furrowed brow)*: Hmm, I didn't know that.

Salesperson: Well, you know just about everything else, so I had to offer something of value! See, here's the same refrigerator in black, model number BOV123B.

Dan: I was concerned that it might be a slightly different refrigerator. I have heard that manufacturers offer slight derivations to certain stores so they can sell them cheaper.

Salesperson: That's exactly right—and that's why it is important to choose a trusted provider for your appliances. ABC Appliances has been in business since 1972. We also provide our own service department where we employ certified Delvon technicians in the unlikely event you have a problem. One of the issues that we hear from customers who made the mistake of buying from an unknown retailer or from a random online source is that they can't get any response when they have a problem. When you purchase at ABC Appliances, you not only know you are buying from a reputable, long-established company, but you also know that we can provide service support when needed. Plus, with our price-matching policy, there is no risk in you finding this same model at a lower price.

In this example, the sales professional surmised that the customer was an Expert by the depth of his research and knowledge of specifics such as the appliance's make and model number. These characteristics are clearly evident given the fact that Dan was carrying a copy of a consumer magazine and walked directly to the *exact model* he was interested in. The salesperson allayed any concerns about the model number by providing tangible evidence to support her explanation. She also addressed a common concern that an Expert has about service after the sale by framing the heritage and certified service technicians while also removing a potential objection by citing their price-matching policy.

Whereas such depth of knowledge and detailed explanation is essential to establishing credibility with the Expert, it would only serve to suck the fun right out of the shopping experience for the Mastermind. For the Mastermind, the entire shopping experience may have been impromptu. It can often begin as a result of a completely unrelated visit to the store:

The Mastermind enters the showroom in search of a replacement grate for her cooking appliance. As she walks into the store, a beautiful kitchen vignette catches her eye.

Audrey (Mastermind): Oh my GOD! This is gorgeous! *(The Mastermind opens the refrigerator door and the inside light slowly brightens from dark to light.)* That's so cool!

Salesperson: I know, right?! It's called theater lighting. So cool!

Audrey: Wow, they sure have changed refrigerators since I last bought one.

Salesperson: Oh, you have no idea! They have air filters now that make sure your ice cubes don't smell like leftover pizza and your leftover pizza doesn't taste like cardboard.

Audrey: Oh my God! I know exactly what you are talking about.

Salesperson: Yeah, it happens because old refrigerators used to cycle the same air from freezer to refrigerator, back and forth, without filtering the air. So the cold freezer air would warm up a little in the fridge. When the air got warmer, it would suck humidity out of the food—hence cardboard pizza. Then the air would go back into the freezer and drop the humidity—voila—pepperoni ice cubes.

Audrey: I'll be damned. I never thought about that.

Salesperson: Now, some manufacturers go so far as to use two compressors, one for the freezer and one for the fridge, to make sure that doesn't happen. It keeps food fresher for a longer period of time, too. Plus, as you noticed, they just look sharper now.

Audrey: Okay, I gotta have this.

Salesperson: Great, let's get that going for you so we can get it into your house before pizza night!

Salesperson *(after ringing up the sale)*: By the way, I see you are carrying a cooking grate. If you think the new refrigerators are cool, wait until you see the cooking appliances . . .

In this exchange, the sales professional piggybacked immediately on the Mastermind's excitement. Rather than overselling the appliance's benefits, the salesperson focused on the one attention-grabbing feature and segued into an interesting story to illustrate the value of today's more technologically advanced refrigerators. He closed aggressively while enthusiasm was high and engaged in suggestive selling *after* the original transaction was completed to avoid creating confusion and chaos to the situation. Closing the sale with the Mastermind consumer at the height of excitement is the best strategy to offset any confusion that can ensue if the Mastermind begins to consider too many options.

Obviously, these examples boil down longer exchanges into brief interactions. The point is that the way a sales professional frames a product or service has a tremendous impact on its perceived value. When we match the frame to our customer's interactive style, we present what we are selling in its best possible light—and avoid interfering with the customer's understanding of the product's benefit.

COMMON OBJECTIONS

As I travel around the world and work with sales professionals from all different types of industries, by far the most common (and dreaded) objection I am told about is *price*. Unless your organization has vowed to offer the most stripped down, basic, discounted offering in your market niche, then someone else will *always* be cheaper. In my opinion, a price objection actually reflects a more complicated concern, one that links directly back to the customer's interactive style. This is very useful in terms of preemptively addressing the objection. If you know why each style objects to price and you have accurately identified the customer's style during rapport building, then you can address potential objections before they are even stated. First, I will explore each style's likely reason for objecting to price; then I will offer a model for navigating a price objection that works for all four interactive styles.

There are typically one or two issues present when a Romantic protests the price. First, the sales professional likely sold the product benefits as a value to the Romantic, rather than as a value to the Romantic's family and friends. Remember: Romantics will generally spend more money on a loved one than on themselves. If the salesperson can establish the benefit of the purchase *for others*, the price resistance tends to dissipate.

Second, Romantics usually don't like to negotiate aggressively. As honor bar negotiators, they hope that the strength of the relationship will guide this part of the sales process and that the sales professional will offer up the best possible deal. If Romantics express a concern about the price, this might indicate that they don't fully trust that the sales professional has their best interests in mind. This reflects a shortcoming in the relationship building that occurred during the establishing rapport step. Although not a fatal development, the sales professional should make a note to change his or her approach with future Romantic customers. It is quite likely that the salesperson failed to spend enough time gaining the Romantic customer's trust and becoming likable. It will be much more difficult to accomplish that at this later point in the process.

Warriors, on the other hand, *love* to negotiate. For them, a price objection simply signals the beginning of the competition. A good strategy is to plan ahead for the inevitable battle over price. If the Warrior is engaged in a negotiation, the deal is already done. They do *not* want to start this process over somewhere else. However, Warriors hate to lose, so there must be a spirited contest that ends with the Warrior getting something in order for this to go well. Even if the sales professional makes a relatively nominal final concession, it is vital that the Warrior prevail. When Warriors do prevail, they will feel good about having won a tough negotiation with a confident and competent opponent.

However, if they lose the negotiation, although they may still purchase the product or service, they will do so with a sour taste in their mouth. Like any competitive person, the Warrior reacts to losing by wanting a rematch—best two out of three. Now, you have created a customer who is looking for an opportunity to even the score. This is not wise. If anything should go wrong with the product or service—which the Warrior will be monitoring closely—then the game is on again, with your Warrior opponent even more motivated than before. Do yourself a favor; let the Warrior customer win something of value that you are comfortable including in the deal.

An Expert's price objection reflects his or her risk aversion. "What if I buy this and discover it cheaper somewhere else or find out that it was not worth it?" Remember, Experts hate mistakes—and overpaying for a product or service is a doozy for them. There are a few strategies you can use to allay this fear, depending on the nature of your industry. Something as simple as going online with the Expert to look at comparable prices can be very reassuring, as can providing some compelling references and testimonials. As they say, there is safety in numbers. Point out policies that ensure satisfaction and money-back guarantees; provide trial test periods and price matching. All of these mitigate risk. The key is to inform the Expert on all the assurances that exist to remove the potential for a mistake.

Of all the styles, Masterminds seem to offer the fewest price objections. If they do, it is more likely a reflection that the product or service hasn't excited them enough to buy it, no matter what the price. Perhaps the sales professional oversold the product, talking past the moment of peak excitement and ultimately sucking the fun right out of the product or service. If so, now would be a good time to return to the origins of the Mastermind interest. Remind the Mastermind of what attracted him or her to the product in the first place. Highlight the cool, unique, or cutting-edge features that the product possesses. It will be important to reinvigorate this sales transaction by regaining the enthusiasm that existed initially. Remember, the Mastermind's interest can depart as quickly as it arrived. *Squirrel!*

HANDLING OBJECTION MODEL

I was doing a sales training seminar in New York a few years back and had been informed that one of the participants was one of the most successful sales professionals in the luxury product space. During the workshop, the attendees completed the same assessment you took in this book. As I often do, I gave the group a break when they completed the assessment, and I meandered around the room checking out the assessment results. (Okay, so I have boundary issues. Sue me!) Anyway, the individual with the luxury sales prowess scored a 12 in the Warrior column. Twelve! That is the highest possible preference for the Warrior style. General George Patton would have probably scored a 14.

As the class continued, I would sneak a glance toward this individual to check out his reaction to the content. He was a tall, lanky 30-something who walked with a swagger and had an obvious love for hair products. Each time I looked over toward him, he seemed fully engaged and receptive. Finally, in the last hour of a full-day class, I introduced my model for handling a customer's concern about a product or service price. After I covered the same model I am about to share with you, Mr. Warrior on Steroids' hand went up.

"Yeah, that model's fine, I guess, and I am sure these guys can benefit by it," Mr. WOS began with a thick Brooklyn accent. "That's not how I do it, and I don't know if you know, but I am the top salesperson in the luxury space for this company."

I nodded. "Yes, I am aware of that, and I would love to hear your approach."

"Well, you're right that these folks will try to pull that price shit . . . um, sorry . . . crap. You know, I have spent about an hour with them and then all the sudden they say, 'Joey, what are you going to do for me. That's a lot of money, Joey. You gotta help me out, Joey.' When they start that, I just say, 'Oh, I'm sorry. I didn't know you don't have no money. Let's find something cheap for you,' and I walk away. You know what? They always pony up then. In fact, sometimes, they buy two just to prove to me that they have the coin!"

I laughed so hard I almost couldn't finish the class. "Well, Joey, when you score a 12 in column d, I guess you can use that approach! I don't have the, um, confidence, to pull that off—so I came up with another approach."

To understand the philosophy behind my model for handling objections, I think it is important to understand the psychology that informs it. Every sales professional has lost a sale because due to failure to overcome a consumer objection. Because all sales professionals are measured by their ability to sell—and because their compensation is very often directly connected to selling—failing to overcome an objection and losing a sale is bad. It is a threat. Psychologically, the loss of a sale is the same as being hit in the head. Both should be avoided. Because of that, a salesperson's natural reaction to a consumer expressing an objection is very similar to how he or she would react to a physical threat.

Think about a time you were driving along in your car, lost in thought, when all of a sudden a police car comes flying up behind you with its lights on and sirens wailing. This is not a physical threat, but you respond physiologically. Your heart rate increases, you perspire, and your mental focus becomes intense—but your intellect diminishes. Your autonomic nervous system is in charge and instructing you to either attack or run. Fight or flight.

A sales professional will have a very similar reaction to a customer who expresses an objection. The salesperson *attacks* (arguing with the customer that his or her objection is not valid) or *runs* (substitutes an inferior product or service at a lower price to try to save the sale). The salesperson's behavior is being driven by the hormonal cocktail featuring cortisol and adrenaline. As if the instinct to fight or flee wasn't bad enough, the salesperson is also much less intelligent in the initial state of this response. While you are intently focused on the perceived threat, you are not intellectually nimble. I mean, does anyone respond to the police car scenario by saying, "Damn, a cop! Oh, I need to pick up some milk, too." (If you are unsure of the impact of the fight or flight response on judgment and intelligence, just watch an episode of *Cops*.)

The good news is that the hormones' impact on intellect ebbs relatively quickly, generally in less than 10 seconds. Now, anyone who has had an argument with his or her spouse knows how dangerous a 10-second reduction in intelligence can be. Haven't we all had our hot button pushed and replied with a remark that got about a foot out of our mouths before our brains screamed, "NOOOOO!" Too late—and suddenly you're left to spend the next 2 hours (or days) apologizing and surfing the Internet for the perfect gift that says, "I am an idiot and I am lucky that you love me."

My model (Figure 6.2) is unique because it addresses the salesperson's natural tendency to want to attack or run—and

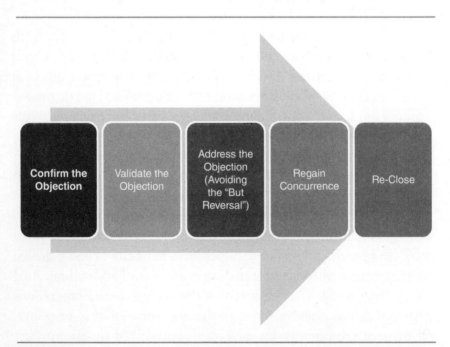

FIGURE 6.2   A Model for Addressing Customer Objections

provides a strategy for working around that initial drop in intellectual capacity. Let's take a look at the model, and I will explain the purpose of each step. As I mentioned, the neat thing about this model is most of the execution is exactly the same regardless of interactive style. There is only one component that changes to address the type of consumer with whom you are working—and that is the section where the customer objection is actually addressed.

Step One: Confirm the Objection

Step Two: Validate the Objection

Step Three: Address the Objection (Avoiding the "But Reversal")

Step Four: Regain Concurrence

Let's examine the purpose of each of step.

Confirm the Objection

Let's build on the early examples of a customer purchasing kitchen appliances, and imagine that the sales professional has attempted a trial close. Perhaps the salesperson said something like, "It sounds like this refrigerator is perfect for your needs. Would you like to set up a home delivery?" The customer responds with, "It's a great refrigerator, but it costs more money than I expected to pay." The customer has offered a price objection. During the confirmation step of the process, the sales professional might respond with, "So what I'm hearing you say is that you love the refrigerator; you are just concerned about the investment. Is that right?"

Consider what you accomplish in this simple reply. First, the sales professional *is not attacking or fleeing*. She is maintaining a consultative approach and remaining aligned with the customer.

Second, the sales professional is maintaining the focus on the product that best meets the consumer's needs, rather than moving backward in the process. Now, if the salesperson has done a poor job of understanding the client's needs, then she may need to back up. If that is the case, more work in asking good questions is necessary. If, however, the salesperson is certain that this is the right refrigerator for the customer based on a successful needs assessment, it is essential that the focus remain on this one appliance.

Third, the salesperson has moved the concept of cost *from price to investment*. Notice the language the salesperson used: This is an important distinction. When a customer is buying a durable good or a luxury item, part of the salesperson's responsibility is to ensure the customer's satisfaction throughout the entire life of the product. A refrigerator should last a decade, and this customer's needs will change in that period of time. If the customer purchases a refrigerator to meet today's needs, it may be not be able to meet the needs of five years from now. When this happens, the consumer is forced to either (1) buy another refrigerator early (before the "life" runs out) or (2) live with an unsatisfactory product for five years. Neither of these options is appealing.

The final issue that is addressed by this simple sentence is that *it allows some time to pass*. Remember, during those first few seconds after the consumer has offered an objection, the sales professional is not at his or her cognitive best. This confirmation gives the salesperson some time for cognition to improve so that this momentary decline in judgment doesn't cause any damage.

Validate the Objection

This step is often the most difficult for sales professionals to apply. It involves them saying something like, "You're right; a new refrigerator is a significant investment. It is a very important decision." When I share step this during sales training seminars, more than half the attendees look at me in horror. "Why would I want to *acknowledge that?*" they say. Well, um, maybe because it is *true!* Particularly as it relates to durable goods and luxury items, the investment is greater and decision is tougher. It is important to understand that and to empathize with your customer. Heck, you can even add, "I remember when I last purchased a refrigerator. I was shocked by how much they had changed in the 10 years since I had shopped for one." Of course, you would say this only if it were true. My point is, consumers are counting on you to be an ally in this process. They need you to validate and potentially empathize with their concerns to reassure them.

Address the Objection (Avoiding the "*But* Reversal")

What? You've never heard of the *but* reversal? Well, it's not a fancy gymnastic move pioneered by the Czech Republic. Nope. In fact, it is probably something you have done many times and created unintended harm. Maybe you have a son who came home from school with a report card that had 2 A's, 2 B's, and 1 D. You said, "Hey, Bobby, you did really great in English and science and pretty good in social studies, but what happened in math?" Or maybe you coach a girls' soccer team and told your daughter that she played a great game, but if she practiced her defense more she'd be even better. Still not sure what the *but* reversal is? Okay, here's an exercise you can do right now at home. Start a fight with your spouse. (I'll wait.)

Okay, now go apologize to your spouse by saying, "I'm sorry, honey, but . . ." I guarantee the fight will not be over and that your spouse will have no memory of the apology later. Why? Because the word *but* is a mind eraser. Nothing survives a *but*. If your boss came up to you at work and said, "Bill, you are a fantastic employee. Everyone here just loves working with you, but . . ." you will have no recollection of the lovely sentiments that preceded the *but*. The same principle is true when handling objections. If you follow your confirmation and validation steps with the word *but*, you have undone all the alignment that you created in those first two steps.

The correct word is to use is *and*. *And* is a more inclusive word. When you use *and*, the other person gets to *keep* all the information that preceded it and is more receptive to what that follows. Try it yourself. Read the following two exchanges, one with *but* and one with *and*, and notice the difference in the feel simply based on changing one tiny word.

Salesperson: It sounds like this refrigerator is perfect for your needs. Would you like to set up a home delivery?

Customer: It's a great refrigerator, but it costs more money than I expected to pay.

Salesperson: So what I'm hearing you say is that you love the refrigerator; you are just concerned about the investment. Is that right?

Customer: Yes, I just didn't expect to pay that much.

Salesperson: You're right; a new refrigerator is a significant investment. It is a very important decision. I remember when I last purchased a refrigerator. I was shocked by how much they had changed in the 10 years since I had shopped for one. **But** it's important to keep in mind the enhancements this appliance will make to your life. The air filtration system alone will pay for itself with a few years.

Now, read the same exchange with one simple word change: *and* instead of *but*.

Customer: It's a great refrigerator, but it costs more money than I expected to pay.

Salesperson: So what I'm hearing you say is that you love the refrigerator; you are just concerned about the investment. Is that right?

Customer: Yes, I just didn't expect to pay that much.

Salesperson: You're right; a new refrigerator is a significant investment. It is a very important decision. I remember when I last purchased a refrigerator. I was shocked at how much they had changed in the 10 years since I had shopped for one. **And** it's important to keep in mind is the enhancements this appliance will make to your life. The air filtration system alone will pay for itself with a few years.

Amazing, isn't it? Simply inserting *and* where you had originally said *but* changes the entire tenor of the conversation. Now put down the book and go apologize to your spouse, correctly this time!

I actually think that the use of the word *and* is even more important than exactly what you say after it. However, it is important to address the objection by reminding the consumer of the value of the product that got the two of you to this point in the negotiation process. Remember, you spent time building rapport, identifying the customer's needs, and framing the value of this product to the customer's specific interactive style. Now you simply need to reinforce that value one more time using the same style approach as before. This means that you remind the Romantic how much this purchase will benefit family and friends. For the Warrior, you reinforce the benefit of the product from both a value (good deal) and status standpoint. The Expert will want to be reminded that this option is reliable and that any investment will be offset by the savings generated by its features. Finally, the Mastermind will respond to a reminder of all the cool and unique qualities that the product possesses.

Regain Concurrence

As you review the attributes of the product or service that appealed to the consumer, remember to add a few rhetorical questions such as, "Does that make sense?" or "Do you see how that would be valuable to you?" These questions, which are often accompanied by the sales professional's head nod, encourage concurrence with the consumer. When the consumer expressed a concern about the product or service, it created a momentary misalignment. We actually started to realign when we confirmed the objection. At that point, we agreed that we weren't aligned by merely ending the confirmation with the question, "Is that right?" It was kind of like agreeing that we aren't agreeing. That is the first step back toward alignment. While we address the consumer's concerns, it is vital that we obtain his or her agreement in our position. Once we believe we have sufficiently regained concurrence, we simply re-close. If the consumer still objects, the process will repeat until all the consumer concerns have been addressed. Oh, and remember to avoid the *but* reversal each time!

The important learning points when it comes to selling to each style are these:

- Use a *consultative approach* to selling.
- Establish rapport with your customer based on *his or her interactive style preference.*
- Once you have established the customer's needs, frame *the product's value* in a way that resonates with that person's style.
- Use a model for handling objections that *quickly realigns* you with the customer.
- Avoid the *but reversal.*

Now let's explore how we can serve each of the different styles as both internal and external customers.

Chapter 7 Providing Customer Service to Each Style

The Key to High Customer Satisfaction Results Is Adjusting to the Customer's Style

Many years ago, when my career in organizational development and training was just starting, I was responsible for new hire training at Marshall Field's—the legendary Chicago-based retailer renowned for its customer service. Marshall Field, the man, had written a book called *Give the Lady What She Wants* and was one of the most influential early figures in retail service excellence. In fact, it was our policy to avoid using the word *no* at all costs when responding to a customer's request. It was during this period in my career that I began to realize just how important internal customer service was to creating a culture of service excellence.

During the new hire training program, we would play a lighthearted video called *If Looks Could Kill*, produced by John Cleese's training company. Despite the fact that I haven't seen that video in more than 25 years, its three primary customer service points have remained indelibly etched in my brain—and continue to inform how I behave. The three points were:

- Behavior breeds behavior.
- You can choose your behavior.
- Positive behavior overcomes negative behavior.

You can construct a darn good service excellence strategy by just focusing in those three concepts. I would add a fourth tenet to make the approach even more powerful:

- Interact with people the way *they* prefer.

Let's examine each of these tenets individually.

BEHAVIOR BREEDS BEHAVIOR

I don't think it is any great revelation that the way we treat others has a huge influence on how they treat us. If we are angry with another, that person typically gets angry back. So if we want to have happy, charming customers, the best strategy would be to treat them in a happy and charming way. Where I think many organizations get off track is in the way they treat their *internal* customers.

You see, when people are treated poorly, the impact of that interaction often extends beyond the immediate relationship. Think about it. If you have a fight with your spouse, don't you find that you may be at least a little less delightful with whomever you interact with next? You might not be angry with *that person*, but you often don't have the same enthusiasm for the conversation because of the previous argument's residual effect.

When we treat our coworkers (internal customers) in a less-than-stellar manner, we create domino effects that will eventually undermine the organization's ability to provide service excellence. That is why it is so essential to treat both our internal and external customers with courtesy and respect.

YOU CAN CHOOSE YOUR BEHAVIOR

This is not easy, but it's true. In fact, the ability to choose your behavior is the core of metacognition. If we engage our meta-cognitive skills and truly *think about how we think*, we can influence our behavior. Unfortunately, as I mentioned in the Introduction, most of us don't challenge our own thought processes. Rather, we cling to our delusion as if it were absolute reality. You must first recognize that you *can* choose your behavior and then make a good choice. It certainly helps if some extrinsic rewards exist in the situation. There is a reason that the best sales professionals are often quite nimble when it comes to adjusting their behavior according to the situation: They get a commission to do so.

POSITIVE BEHAVIOR OVERCOMES NEGATIVE BEHAVIOR

I believe this. I truly think everyone wants to be happy. There is no doubt that some people are more committed to negativity than others. You know who I am talking about—the Debbie Downers of the world. (As my dad used to say, "Some people are born ugly, live ugly, and die ugly.") However, this is a fairly small percentage of the population—and Lord knows what has happened to them to put them in this state. The overall majority of people *far* prefer being in a good mood to the alternative. So when you choose to be upbeat and supportive in the face of an upset customer, you have the leverage on your side.

INTERACT WITH PEOPLE THE WAY THEY PREFER

This is the component of service that distinguishes excellence from competence. In my opinion, the ability to be courteous and deliver service that meets the customer's expectation is the *basic requirement* of an organization. I do not applaud that effort; I expect it. The value-add in the area of customer service—the embodiment of service *excellence*—comes when customer service is delivered in the specific way *that particular* customer prefers it to be delivered. That means the service provider must recognize the customer's behavioral cues and adjust the approach to service delivery accordingly. Let's look at how you do this with each style.

SERVING THE ROMANTIC

A genuine smile will go a long way to endear you to the Romantic. It is an immediate show of friendship and warmth. Even if you are interacting on the phone, a smile traverses the airwaves and finds its way into the Romantic's heart. Because Romantics are the most loyal of consumers, recognizing them and *using their name* is also critical. Showing appreciation for their business and remembering some elements of their life and preferences works very powerfully as well. Spending some time getting to know internal customers personally will make the relationship more meaningful. Romantics try to create emotionally stable and supportive environments, so anything you can do to contribute to that effort will be viewed as positive. Above all else, remember to appreciate them (sincerely!) for their patronage (external customers) or efforts (internal customers).

As a Romantic myself, I am a sucker for a service provider who exhibits a warm, sincere smile and treats me with the familiarity of an old friend. I reward such service with loyalty and return time and again to those shops, restaurants, and hotels. Romantic consumers, when treated well, are the best retention market around.

SERVING THE WARRIOR

Get a result! Warrior customers value people who can get things done quickly. Anything you can do to resolve an issue in an expedient way will impress the Warrior. The Warrior customer prefers to work with someone who is confident. As a secondary Warrior, I find myself behaving in this style from time to time. As a former colleague told me, "One thing I learned from working with you is to tell you what I *did*, not what I am planning to do." Internal Warrior customers like to know that you are a resource for making their job easier, not a black hole of red tape. Help Warrior customers navigate their situation without unnecessary details and delay, and you will delight them. If the Warrior knows you can be trusted to get things done without being micromanaged (and vice versa), then the Warrior will rest assured.

As a secondary Warrior, I pay attention to things such as the ease of the transaction. I am much happier when things are expedient, make sense, and flow logically. If there appears to be inefficiencies in the process or if the wait to acquire service is too long, my service needs are not being met. The mere existence of a line, say at a hotel check-in desk, tests the patience of Warriors.

SERVING THE EXPERT

Listen to what an Expert has to say. This may take some time, but it is important to the Expert customer that you understand everything related to the situation he or she is in. Provide accurate information, and remember than everything you say is an implied promise. If you give the Expert a time frame, make sure you meet that expectation. Keep your appointments, and be trustworthy. You need be a source of reliable data and performance for internal Expert customers. Be consistent and help them reduce any chance of a mistake. If you have knowledge, share it with them. Expert customers will feel more secure knowing that they can count on you to deliver exactly as you have told them you will.

Remember, Experts value *what they know to be true.* As you continually deliver on your service promise, you build more credibility with Experts. It is more important to manage expectations and ensure that Experts experience service consistent with what they have been told; do not make aggressive statements about your capabilities and then fall short. Make one mistake in serving Experts, and your reputation may be forever tarnished. Be honest, accurate, and reliable, and Experts will grant you their highest reward: *trust.* Personally, Experts have pushed me to think more deeply about specific logistics, training deliverables, and details. They have made me a better service provider.

SERVING THE MASTERMIND

You must provide Masterminds with a creative way to solve their problems. Mastermind customers like knowing that they are working with someone who is not encumbered by precedent, policy, and procedure when it comes to devising a solution. They love people who are excited by the challenge of satisfying the unique demands they share. Maintaining your enthusiasm and optimism is exhilarating to Masterminds, particularly when they are engaged in brainstorming. Indulge their ideas, and give each one consideration regardless of their feasibility—because it is in the exploration of concepts that some form of genius can occur.

Be very wary of telling Masterminds no. *No* is a dangerous word to *any* interactive style in that it ends your value to a customer; however, it's particularly damaging to your service relationship with a Mastermind because it ends the options. Rather than saying no, offer two or three options that you *can* achieve. You will be amazed at how quickly the Mastermind moves in another, more mutually acceptable direction.

Life is an adventure for Masterminds. They want their service providers to be able to respond to their unique needs and, at the very least, to share their enthusiasm for the possibilities. I am often surprised at what can be achieved when you provide open-minded customer service to Masterminds. I have developed entire programs simply by giving full consideration to the service exceptions that a Mastermind has requested. So embrace the potential they offer.

LAST MODEL OF SERVICE RECOVERY

No matter how adept we are or become at metacognition and situationally adjusting our interactive style, we will occasionally encounter a customer (internal or external) who is not pleased with us—or the organization we represent. For these situations, I suggest the LAST model of service recovery: listen, apologize, solve, and thank. It is a simple model, but it is hugely effective.

Listen

Listening to the concerns of another person is easy, right? Well, not really. You may hear some things that you deem inaccurate and feel compelled to immediately set the record straight. Or, as a service provider, you probably know exactly how to fix the problem long before the other party is done telling you the story. But understanding the other person's point of view is actually only *part* of the reason that you listen to his or her perspective. Of course, it is absolutely necessary to fully understand the customer's concern, but another important reason for listening to the entire customer story is to allow the other party to, ahem, empty his or her CTL container.

You remember the CTL (crap tolerance level) container, right? We discussed that in Chapter 1, which focused on the differences between Romantics and Warriors. *Venting*, the more professional description for this concept, is very important during service recovery. It is essential that the other party feel as though he or she has gotten all the stored-up frustrations out in the open before that person is ready to evaluate the solutions you will offer.

One way to tell whether your customer is done venting is by listening for a change in tone. During the initial part of this step, the customer may be upset, frustrated, or at least irritated, using language that is full of aggressive and/or accusatory words and phrases. As you continue to listen, you will hear the tone become less aggressive, perhaps even culminating with something like, "I know it's not your fault, but I am just really frustrated by this situation." It is at this moment that the venting is complete.

Apologize

There is nothing so disarming as an apology. Anyone married more than a year knows that every marital spat is more about who will apologize rather than who is right or wrong. Once an apology has been offered, there is an implication that responsibility has been accepted and the two parties can now move toward problem solving. Given that "the customer is always right," it makes very little sense to prolong the argument over accountability. For this reason, as soon as the customer has completely vented, you should offer a genuine and sincere apology.

Now, saying, "I'm sorry you have experienced this" is not the same thing as saying, "It is my fault you are upset." That is an important distinction. The apology allows both parties to progress to solution mode; it does not establish culpability. I am of the camp that it doesn't matter who is at fault; what matters is that we fix the problem and avoid it in the future. The apology pushes us past blame focus and on to solution focus. I do realize that this is easier said than done. Apologizing to someone who has just expressed frustration, perhaps in a loud and aggressive way, can be very challenging. Do it anyway.

Solve

If you can fix the problem in the exact way that your customer demands, then this step is pretty easy. Fix it. However, in many circumstances, the customer's demands may exceed the service provider's authority. Let me eliminate one option for you right now. *Never say no.* I have never seen the "no" option work with *any* interactive style. When you tell a customer no, you have essentially removed any value you have to the customer. If you have no value, the customer is left with two options: find someone who has more authority, or never work with you and your organization again.

The latter option is obviously problematic, particularly for internal customers. How can we offer service excellence to our colleagues when they believe we have no value and choose not to work with us? The first option invites the customer to seek out your boss. Um, your boss doesn't want to deal with a problem that you can't fix—and, by the way, your boss generally ends up giving the customer the exact solution to which you said no. Now you have a dynamic where the customer doesn't respect you, your boss doesn't respect you, you don't respect your boss, and you resent the customer. Yeah, that sounds like a good endgame.

Now, never saying no is *not* the same as always saying yes. As mentioned when dealing with Masterminds, always provide options. Instead of saying, "No, I can't do that," say, "Here are a few ways we can solve that problem. Which of these is the most appealing to you?" Most people will pick the option that they find best meets their needs. In the event you have a customer whose continued demands exceed your authority, simply say,

"Let me see what I can do" and then discuss the situation with your boss. The key is to *maintain a position of value* with your client so he or she is not forced to circumvent you.

Thank

Remember how hard apologizing to an unhappy customer was? Well, try thanking the person. I mean, how weird is to thank someone who, at best, expressed disappointment in the service received and, at worst, may have been upset enough to *yell* at you? Why in the world would we want to thank someone after enduring this? The simple answer is this: They did you a favor. In this day of social media and instant, broad communication potential, an unhappy customer can post concerns on any number of websites without having ever given you the opportunity to fix the problem. When I read online reviews of restaurants, I often wonder if these people expressed their dissatis-faction to management while they were at the establishment. My bet is that they sat quietly, said nothing, and let their fingers do the talking when they returned home. I also bet that had they asked to speak to the manager while at the restaurant, they may well have had a different experience. The point is that those customers who are courageous enough to address their concerns to you and not behind the cloak of anonymity deserve our appreciation. Thank them for allowing us to correct their concerns.

Let me just add this on the subject of social media. An entire book could be written on how each style uses these resources—and perhaps I will tackle that topic in my next one. But for now, here is something interesting and maybe a bit counterintuitive to consider. Romantics don't like conflict and often are unlikely to express their concerns in person. They are, however, very comfortable sharing their concerns with others—and this very possibly includes using social media outlets. Hell hath no fury like a Romantic scorned, so to speak. For this reason, I encourage you to be particularly assertive in getting feedback from Romantics. If they are not happy, allow them plenty of safe, nonconfrontational avenues for sharing their concerns with you. And don't just fix these problems when they share them; *show your appreciation* emphatically for the Romantic consumer's input. The only thing more impressive to the Romantic than excellent service is excellent service recovery.

And there you have it. Listen, apologize, solve, and thank. It's really very simple. Well, certainly simple in theory. The key is to execute it effectively under duress. Service recovery can be emotionally charged, so having a simple model for navigating these choppy waters is very helpful.

Chapter 8 Personal Relationships and Interactive Style

Better Understand Family and Friends and Enhance Your Marriage

I mentioned earlier a curious observation when it comes to love: There appears to be a good many marriages and romantic couplings of all types that involve two partners that, in any other dynamic, would appear to be completely incompatible. Somehow, when romance is added to the equation, interactive style takes a backseat . . . well, at least initially. There is most definitely an initial stage of romantic partnership that is more hormonal than style-driven. But what does one do when that early euphoria of love gives way to a more potentially enduring, or destructive, next phase? The answer lies in understanding those intrinsic needs, respecting the diverse contribution of each person to the partnership, and having a well-established process for resolving the inevitable conflict.

Romantics thrive in environments that are abundant with appreciation for the sacrifices they make for others. Genuine, sincere sharing of love and gratitude will go a long way in fulfilling their needs. They don't *ask* for this appreciation, at least not in overt ways that styles like the Warrior or the Expert may notice, so it is important that a Romantic's partner regularly provide evidence of appreciation, even if the Romantic doesn't seem to need it.

The feeling component of the environment is also critical to a Romantic's contentment. Although Romantics will occasionally have a need to vent (and it will be important for their partner to develop the listening skills of a good venting outlet), they prefer to experience a more stable, upbeat, and compassionate atmosphere. The foundation of marital satisfaction for Romantics is having a partner who contributes to a home with *positive emotional content*. Romantics who are constantly trying to lift others' spirits and overcome negative emotional barriers will eventually become weary of the eternal buzzkill that is their own household. Even Romantics need care for the caregiver.

Warriors measure life through a prism of time/value ratio. They evaluate any invested time relative to the perceived value of the activity. So when a great deal of time is invested, a great deal of value is expected. For this reason, Warriors often apply pressure on others or situations to reduce the time required and therefore the value required. Warriors avoid activities (and people) that appear to have no significant value. They also are not particularly keen on others meddling in their affairs.

Warriors will be happiest in a marital situation that allows for efficient decisions, good planning, and a life strategy that clearly achieves their goals as rapidly as possible. They thrive in a romantic dynamic where both parties can operate independently with a common vision and where this clarity supersedes the need for unnecessary or repetitive discussions. Having clearly delineated authority and providing each other their scope of influence makes sense to Warriors. By operating in this fashion,

Warriors experience the independence within which they thrive and the ability to pursue the goal to which they aspire, all in the most expeditious of ways.

Slow and steady wins the race for Experts. More accurately (and Experts love accuracy), cautious and compliant wins the race. Experts build a happy partnership on agreed-upon rules and expectations. The environment is stable, reliable, and repeatable. There is security in the routines and comfort in the familiarity. The Expert needs to know that his or her partner is someone who can be depended on and whose behavior remains constant throughout all situations.

Unnecessary changes or risk taking, at least as perceived by the Expert, are unnerving. When it's time to make decisions, the issues should be well researched and discussed at length. Questions will need to be asked and answered to ensure that the Expert has carefully and thoroughly evaluated the merits of each potential action. Allowing the Expert to protect the household from the chaos of mistakes provides a sense of purpose and respect that feeds his or her intrinsic needs.

Masterminds hate boredom. The routines and monotony of a long-term marriage may take a toll on them if effort isn't expended to keep things exciting. Unique activities, unconventional hobbies, unusual vacations, and changes in their surroundings can all reignite their enthusiasm. They love to experience new, cool, and intriguing experiences and are always evaluating the potential of ideas to which they are exposed.

A Mastermind's partner should be prepared to be "up for anything." Indulging the Mastermind's whims and acting on his or her impulses will create a dynamic of two explorers navigating unknown waters. The key is to create a romance that is the living embodiment of "Never a dull moment." Because not all ideas will work out, Masterminds also thrive within an environment that is forgiving of the occasional mistake. They know that with risk comes failure. It is how Masterminds learn, and they live by the motto, "Nothing ventured, nothing gained."

Sometimes something ventured will result in nothing gained other than an important life lesson. But for the Mastermind, that's enough.

CONFLICT RESOLUTION

Conflict is unavoidable. We are all uniquely delusional, so there is absolutely no way to prevent uncomfortable interactions with others. On this level, my dad was exactly right when he said, "The world would be a wonderful place if it weren't for people." No matter how well you learn the lessons this book imparts, some people will still irritate you. What's important is that we have a positive and constructive model for resolving conflict when it occurs. The source of conflict is often rooted in the difference in interactive styles between two people. I try to operate with the point of view that everyone's behavior makes perfect sense to that person, even if it doesn't to me. In the Introduction, I used the example of two different reactions to a stray dog. The dog exists as absolute reality, but the *perception* of the dog is determined through the subjectivity of our schemas.

The same can be said about human behavior. How someone behaves may have been intended to be one thing but perceived quite differently by another. In this way, conflict resolution is really about seeking to understand a broader truth beyond your own perception of an experience. (Whoa, that's a pretty highfalutin sentence for me.) Essentially, the pursuit of conflict resolution boils down to believing that the other person's behavior makes sense to that person. You just have to figure out why.

Some common sources of conflict can be traced directly to interactive style. For example, Romantics are often irritated by Warriors' direct communication style. They may perceive the words as being overly blunt, even harsh. Romantics may interpret this style as angry, even when the Warrior is not. And as we know, Romantics get upset when they feel unappreciated. They enter into conflict when they believe the other party failed to be empathetic, sympathetic, or compassionate toward them—or others, for that matter. They prefer harmony and consensus, two things that are far less important to Warriors (and even Experts and Masterminds).

Romantics may engage in some toxic coping mechanisms rather than using healthy conflict resolutions—for example, placing their frustrations inside their CTL container. They might also display passive-aggressive tendencies by discussing their concerns with others who are not directly involved in the conflict or feigning agreement when they, in fact, do not agree.

Warriors more commonly find themselves in conflict with Experts. This generally has to do with Experts' need to share details and explain things thoroughly. As I illustrated with the examples of e-mails in Chapter 4 on recognizing each style, Warriors prefer a more bottom line, bullet point approach to communication. They also like to get to the decision rather than endure an exhaustive discussion of all the data. Experts, conversely, prefer to share the entire context so that you understand completely the dynamic, an approach that places them squarely on the wrong side of the time/value ratio. The toxic strategies that Warriors deploy include becoming more autocratic ("because I said so"), refusing to share information (to avoid "unnecessary" discussion), or lashing out at Experts to shut them down.

The Mastermind's bouncing brain can madden Experts. Because Experts like to approach issues in a linear way and work through them from start to finish, they find the Mastermind's tendency toward tangents frustrating. Experts approach all interactions as if they were driven by a clear agenda that outlines what we will tackle first, second, third, and so on. Masterminds operate in a more freewheeling way. At a minimum, Experts may view this as a distraction. Potentially, they may see Masterminds as lacking focus, being uncommitted, or even being airheads. Experts may exhibit toxic behaviors such as stubbornly refusing to consider the Mastermind's ideas, ignoring the Mastermind's input, or blaming the Mastermind for sabotaging the discussion.

I often joke that the Mastermind is the one style that is not irritated by one of the others. You know why? They aren't paying any attention. "What's that annoying sound? Oh, Bob's still talking." I do think there is potential for Masterminds to become annoyed by Romantics' desire for consensus. If Masterminds have what they believe to be a good idea, they are not likely to need or desire others' approval; meanwhile, Romantics would be prone to "run this by" a few people to get buy-in. In such scenarios, the Mastermind might decide to go rogue and engage in activities without all the appropriate approval. The Mastermind may also brand the Romantic as a malcontent, not committed to the vision. Or the Mastermind may give up on the idea completely because the process of achieving consensus is time-consuming and boring.

Keep in mind that any style can have conflict with any style, including someone with the same style. But no matter with whom you're clashing, the following model effectively resolves conflict—provided that both parties follow the guidelines.

A MODEL FOR CONFLICT RESOLUTION

To successfully resolve a conflict, each party must operate within a certain set of guidelines. Following are the rules of engagement.

- There must be a *genuine desire between both parties to understand the other's perspective.* The presumption is that each party believes that his or her perspective is correct and that the behaviors that led to the conflict were not malicious in intent. If so, then the purpose of the process is to better understand the issue and to broaden our knowledge. If you do not have a sincere interest in the other party's point of view, then there really is no reason to even try to resolve the conflict. Remember, conflict resolution is not about determining right or wrong. Such an attempt will only result in an argument. Conflict resolution is about pursuing the *broader understanding* of an issue.

- The conflict *is about an issue, not a person.* All comments will be related to how each perceived the specific behaviors that created the rift and will not be directed at the person(s) involved. For example, using *you* likely indicates that you are indicting the other person's motives, rather than focusing on your own perceptions of the situation. When a person in conflict tells the other party, "You were disrespectful," for example, that person is expressing a misguided sense of surety about the other person's intent. Doing so is very inflammatory to the other. The effect of this language is akin to taking your index finger and pressing it repeatedly into the sternum of the other person. If you are not sure what response that elicits, then take a field trip to your nearest neighborhood drinking establishment, walk up to any patron sitting at the bar, and pop the person in the sternum with your index finger a few times. Yeah, not good! Rather than use *you* language, focus on the *I* perspective. "I felt disrespected" is accurate; "You were disrespectful" is not necessarily true.

- *Don't wait too long* to engage in conflict resolution, but *be mindful of your emotional* state before beginning. Waiting more than about 48 hours increases the risk that you will instead place the conflict in your CTL container, particularly if you are a Romantic. The conflict is not resolved in this case; it is simply delayed and will reemerge later in a more complicated and severer incarnation. On the other hand, if you are upset, angry, or hurt, it is very difficult to maintain the proper composure to discuss the issue effectively. Calm down, but remain committed to resolving any lingering conflict soon.

- No matter how tempting, *keep your conflict between the two of you.* It is very easy to vent your frustration about a situation to another person. Although it is cathartic for you, it can be damaging to the relationship you have with the person with whom you have the conflict. It can even create a new conflict between your confidant and the person with whom you are having conflict. Once we clear up our conflict, we often come away with a better appreciation of *why* the person who once frustrated us so did, said what was said, or behaved the way he or she did. But rarely do people go back to their trusted confidant(s) and clarify the previous discussion. That manufactured conflict between your confidant and former nemesis never gets resolved. Heck, your confidant may even further perpetuate this "conflict viral infection" by sharing it with even more people. When others get involved, the damage can be uncontainable.

- Keep in mind that *the other party may have no idea that a conflict exists*. In fact, this is the most common scenario. Be prepared for the other party to be a little defensive when you begin. This is normal. For that reason, it is a good idea to start the conversation with some reassuring words. If you are resolving conflict with a coworker, you might begin with something like, "I have a great deal of respect for you and really enjoy working together . . ." Just be careful about that next word. Remember the *but* reversal? Same rules apply here. The next word should be *and*. "I have a great deal of respect for you and really enjoy working together, and I wanted to discuss something that happened yesterday that confused me." Again, the use of the word *and* rather than *but* keeps the two of you aligned and keeps the other party more open to your perspective.

- Engage in *active listening*. Maintain eye contact, nod encouragingly, and *do not respond immediately* to anything you hear that you believe is inaccurate. Allow the other party to share his or her entire perspective without passing judgment or interrupting to clarify. This can be really difficult if the other party starts engaging in the aforementioned *you* language, but stay strong. Again, the purpose is to hear the other party's point of view. You may not agree with it, but you do want to *understand* it. The key is for both parties to have uninterrupted time to express their perspectives.

- Once both parties have expressed their perspective, *identify the critical issue(s) that have created the conflict*. I think it is useful to actually write these things down on a piece of paper. By doing so, you can shift the focus of the conflict resolution away from the two people involved and over to the piece of paper. This helps depersonalize the process and realign the two people around a common goal—addressing the issue(s). In fact, I will go so far as to say, if you can reduce the conflict to a few issues on a piece of paper, resolution will come fast.

- Discuss what *future behaviors will be needed by* **both** parties to resolve this conflict. It is best if both parties make commitments to future behaviors. Be sure that you end the process in agreement and on a positive note. Thank the other party for being supportive of the conflict resolution process. If you have talked for more than 30 minutes and have not yet arrived at a resolution, agree to another time in the very near future to readdress the issue(s).

- *Keep your promises* to each other!

- When you find yourself in a particularly sticky conflict during which one or both parties have dug in their heels on the issue, you can try forced empathy. I think of forced empathy as the global thermonuclear war remedy. It requires that each of the two parties in conflict explain the other's perspective, an approach that's especially effective when one party is not listening. When required to explain the other's point of view, each person is required to listen and understand. Once the point of view is understood, the person often sees the validity in that perspective—even if he or she still doesn't entirely agree. That's progress. Also, when you hear your perspective shared by another person who doesn't have the same level of commitment to it, it can become less convincing. These two developments can be just enough to bridge the conflict chasm.

Nobody enjoys conflict, regardless of interactive style (although Warriors seem to take some pleasure in a good old debate). The most courageous component to resolving differences is taking the first step. By the time you get halfway through the steps listed here, things become pretty easy. The most important—and difficult—thing to do is to have that initial conversation.

Also keep in mind that you will get better with more practice. Remember when you first learned to ride a bicycle? You fell off. In fact, you probably fell several times before you built your confidence. Eventually, you became so good at riding a bike that you didn't have to think about it at all. The key to mastering any skill is repetition. The more you engage in conflict resolution, the better you will become. Imagine how much less stressful your life would be if you felt comfortable resolving conflict with others. You just have to get on that bike, fall a few times, and remain committed to the ride.

Conclusion

The Unusual Goal of an Educator

I love delivering *The Power of Understanding People* to my clients in all kinds of industries all around the world. To see the epiphany on the faces of my audience members is incredibly fulfilling. I have received countless e-mails from leaders, sales professionals, and service providers telling me how much the information has enhanced them professionally. Even more gratifying are the numerous correspondences I receive from attendees who have given the assessment to their spouses and benefited from the ensuing conversation.

Within this book, we have learned about the concepts of metacognition and interactive style. You took an assessment to discover the four iconic interactive styles—Romantic, Warrior, Expert, and Mastermind—and how they combine to determine your Hollywood movie character. We learned how to recognize and adjust to each style and apply this information when leading, selling, and servicing each. We even discussed ways to use this information with friends and family. For me, learning this information has enhanced my role as a professional, a husband, a father, and a friend. As an educator, my fondness for sharing it with others is among the most gratifying elements of my life.

It occurred to me several years ago that the job of an educator is largely to create stupidity. Seriously! Here's what I mean. Most of us (including myself!) spend our time operating with the assumption that others will behave in a way that conforms to what we expect. When they don't, we become irritating. We are baffled by miscommunication, confused by unexpected behaviors, and maddened by what we perceive as bad judgment. Even if we know that everyone is different, the first time someone proves it is very aggravating. In other words, we live in a state of unconscious incompetence. They don't know what they don't know. We are clueless as to the impact of metacognition and interactive style.

During my seminars, people have that moment. Their faces light up and they say, "Oh *wow!* That explains my husband." In that precise instant, they have moved from unconscious incompetence to conscious competence. They *know* they don't know. They have become stupid. Stupid is huge. Stupid is the cornerstone of learning. A person cannot master a skill until first recognizing that *a skill exists to be learned*. In my opinion, moving a learner from clueless to stupid is the most important accomplishment of an educator. (It's *really* difficult to market that, though. "Hello, Executive Vice President of Sales. My name is Dave Mitchell, and if you give me your team for just 3 hours, I will make them stupid." Would you hire me?)

So, as a reader, I hope you have enjoyed the book. I hope that you took away valuable insights about yourself. I hope you have started on the path to enhancing your professional and personal relationships. I hope I have made you stupid! Now your journey to better understanding people takes you down the path of applications. Pay attention to others' behaviors. Adjust your approach based on their preferred interactive style. Resolve conflict with a sincere desire to understand the other person's perspective. And remember: Don't test the Invisible Fence on yourself.

Index

NOTE: Page references in italics refer to illustrations.